DETROIT PUBLIC LIBRARY

3 5674 02641664 5

P9-DDB-737

DETROIT PUBLIC LIBRARY
CHASE BRANCH LIBRARY
17731 W. Seven Mile Rd.
Detroit, MI 48235

DATE DUE

OCT 0 5 1998

FEB 2 5 1999

FEB 2 8 2001

BC-3

CH

MAR 1 4 1998

We Changed the World

AFRICAN AMERICANS
1945–1970

THE YOUNG OXFORD HISTORY OF
AFRICAN AMERICANS

Robin D. G. Kelley and Earl Lewis
General Editors

We Changed the World

◇ ◇ ◇

AFRICAN AMERICANS
1945–1970

Vincent Harding
Robin D. G. Kelley
Earl Lewis

Oxford University Press
New York • Oxford

*In memory of Sue Bailey Thurman (1903–1996),
who carried so much of the world-changing
spirit in her own soul, but who couldn't wait
around for this work to be done*

Oxford University Press

Oxford New York
Athens Auckland Bangkok Bogotá Bombay
Buenos Aires Calcutta Cape Town Dar es Salaam Delhi
Florence Hong Kong Istanbul Karachi
Kuala Lumpur Madras Madrid Melbourne
Mexico City Nairobi Paris Singapore
Taipei Tokyo Toronto
and associated companies in
Berlin Ibadan

Copyright © 1997 by Vincent Harding, Robin D. G. Kelley, and Earl Lewis
Introduction copyright © 1997 by Oxford University Press

Published by Oxford University Press, Inc.,
198 Madison Avenue, New York, New York 10016

Oxford is a registered trademark of Oxford University Press

All rights reserved. No part of this publication
may be reproduced, stored in a retrieval system, or transmitted,
in any form or by any means, electronic, mechanical,
photocopying, recording, or otherwise, without the prior
permission of Oxford University Press.

Design: Sandy Kaufman
Layout: Leonard Levitsky
Picture research: Lisa Kirchner, Martin Baldessari
Library of Congress Cataloging-in-Publication Data
Harding, Vincent.
We changed the world: African Americans, 1945–1970 / Vincent Harding.
p. cm. — (The young Oxford history of African Americans; v. 9)
Includes bibliographical references and index.
1. Afro-Americans—History—1877–1964—Juvenile literature.
2. Afro-Americans—History—1964– —Juvenile literature.
3. Afro-Americans—Civil rights—Juvenile literature.
[1. Afro-Americans—History—1877–1964
2. Afro-Americans—History—1964– 3. Afro-Americans—Civil rights.]
I. Title. II. Series.
E185.Y68   1995   vol. 9
[E185.61]
973'.0496073—dc21   96-52146
CIP
AC

ISBN 0-19-508796-8 (library ed.); ISBN 0-19-508502-7 (series, library ed.)

1 3 5 7 9 8 6 4 2

Printed in the United States of America
on acid-free paper

On the cover: Challenge—America, 1964 by Lois Mailou Jones
Frontispiece: Black citizens picket the school board office in St. Louis, Missouri, in 1963.
Page 9: Detail from *The Contribution of the Negro to Democracy in America* (1943) by Charles White, 11'9" x 17'3"
Hampton University Museum, Hampton, Virginia

CONTENTS

Robin D. G. Kelley
Earl Lewis

INTRODUCTION
◇ ◇ ◇

F rom the earliest days of the earliest colonies in North America, people of African descent in the United States have fought for their rights. Their names—men, women, and children of courage—are therefore permanently etched into the nation's history. You know some of them: Olaudah, Crispus, Paul, Phillis, Harriet, Sojourner, David, Nat, Frederick, Ida, Marcus, and Mary. Often they are connected to the last names Equiano, Attucks, Cuffe, Wheatley, Tubman, Truth, Walker, Turner, Douglass, Wells, Garvey, and Bethune. They and scores of others insisted that African Americans be treated as full and equal citizens.

Yet for all of the continuity in African-American history, including the long history of struggle, the years between 1945 and 1970 represented a new moment. It was a time of new possibilities and a new vision. Black Americans were determined to be the architects of an inclusive America, one that championed human rights for all. They, therefore, openly linked local efforts to global conditions. The fight for economic and racial justice in Baton Rouge, Montgomery, and other Southern towns and cities became part of a worldwide fight for human rights. In song, word, and deed, anticolonial efforts in Africa became connected to human rights struggles in the United States; opposition to the war in Vietnam became linked to the oppression of Third World peoples everywhere. In that sense the black struggle in the United States became a beacon for the world. It allowed activists to say in a loud voice or in hushed tones, "We changed the world."

6

They were aided by the fact that World War II had exposed the persistent contradictions between the American ideal and the American reality. Black Americans resolved to eliminate that contradiction. They would not only fight for democracy abroad; they would pursue democracy at home. In communities large and small they organized after the war, often aided by veterans who had resolved to return home and change things. This new generation of activists joined an earlier generation. Together they used home-grown institutions such as churches, fraternal orders, and civil rights organizations to funnel their efforts. In the cadences of black ministers, the lyrics of gospel and civil rights songs, the energies of college students, and the noble dreams of ordinary folk, they plotted their strategies.

Lest it be forgotten, however, it took community organizing and mobilizing; it took poor and middle class, young and old, the college-educated and school dropouts to organize for social change. Some people resisted, fearing beatings, job loss, and even murder. And for good reason. African Americans who organized the civil rights movement experienced the range of negative response. After all, the federal government only reluctantly backed civil rights workers, and it aggressively investigated black leaders when they complained about the war in Vietnam as well as a range of social inequities at home.

At no time, however, was there just one black American or black America. African Americans often disagreed over strategies, procedures, and timing. Southern activists, for instance, came to realize that the challenges faced by Northern and Western urban dwellers required new emphases. Members of the Student Nonviolent Coordinating Committee (SNCC) publicly and quietly feuded with elders in organizations such as the NAACP and the Southern Christian Leadership Conference (SCLC). Some veterans of interracial cooperation rejected or approached with some caution those who embraced various expressions of Black Power.

What this book shows in dramatic detail is how a postwar generation of African Americans added their names to the pantheon of black heroes and heroines who made and changed America. After 1970 the names Emmett, Thurgood, Medgar, Martin, Ella, Malcolm, Stokely, Bob, Diane, John, Ralph, Fannie, and Septima joined the long list of those who had previously changed the world. This book celebrates their memories by forcing us to confront their deeds. It portrays average human beings who seized their moment to begin another. It is the history of the fight for civil and human rights in post–World War II America. It is the story of the nation's most persistent workers for the expansion of democracy, including those who gave their lives in the quest for "a more perfect union." It is the story of a critical chapter in African-American history.

This book is part of an 11-volume series that narrates African-American history from the 15th through the 20th centuries. Since the 1960s, a rapid explosion in research on black Americans has significantly modified previous understanding of that experience.

National Guardsmen confront marchers on Beale Street, Memphis, in 1968.

Studies of slavery, African-American culture, social protest, families, and religion, for example, silenced those who had previously labeled black Americans insignificant historical actors. The new research followed a general upsurge of interest in the social and cultural experiences of the supposedly powerless men and women who did not control the visible reins of power. The result has been a careful and illuminating portrait of how ordinary people make history and serve as the architects of their own destinies.

This series explores many aspects of the lives of African Americans. It describes how black people shaped and changed the history of this nation. It also places the lives of African Americans in the context of the Americas as a whole. We start the story more than a century before the day in 1619 when 19 "negars" stepped off a slave ship in Jamestown, Virginia, and end with the relationship between West Indian immigrants and African Americans in large urban centers like New York in the late 20th century.

At the same time, the series addresses a number of interrelated questions: What was life like for the first Africans to land in the Americas? Were all Africans and African Americans enslaved? How did race shape slavery and how did slavery influence racism? The series also considers questions about male-female relationships, the forging of African-American communities, religious beliefs and practices, the experiences of the young, and the changing nature of social protest. The key events in American history are here, too, but viewed from the perspective of African Americans. The result is a fascinating and compelling story of nearly five centuries of African-American history.

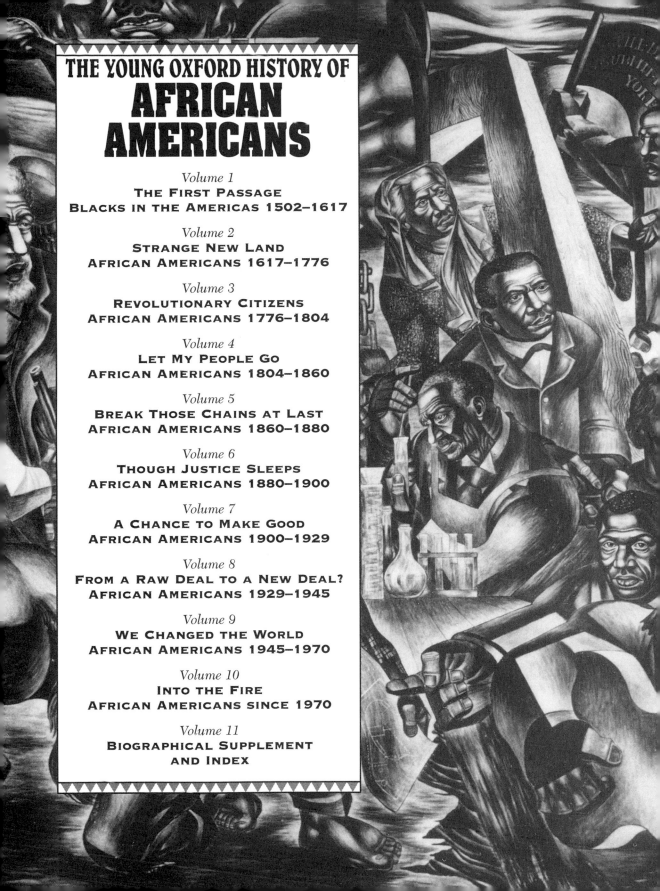

THE YOUNG OXFORD HISTORY OF
AFRICAN AMERICANS

PROLOGUE

The history of African Americans is filled with many ironies, but perhaps at no time was that irony more vividly at work than during the brutal and destructive years of World War II (1939–45). During that conflict, African Americans helped win victory over the white supremacist Nazis, only to return to a land where racism still prevailed. More than all the other wars before it, that global conflict brought untold death and horror to millions of human beings. But at the same time, it created hope and resistance and new opportunities for colonized peoples of color all over the world.

From the moment of their reluctant entrance into the war against Hitler's Germany and his brutally expansionist, anti-Jewish agenda, the western Allies (especially France, England, and the United States) helped to develop the irony. They identified their central purpose as a war against the racism of the Nazis and a war for human freedoms. But, at the same time, France and England were the world's major colonial powers, dominating the lives of millions of people of color in Africa, Asia, and the Caribbean. A commitment to white supremacy was central to their colonial agendas. Deepening the irony was the fact that as the war took its toll on the lives of their own young men, both France and England recruited men from their far-flung colonies, forcing them to fight for a set of freedoms that did not apply to them. These blatant contradictions were not lost on the men who came from the colonies to the killing fields of Europe. Indeed, before the war was over many of these darker veterans were leading the anticolonial movements in their homelands in Africa and Asia. Challenging Europe's moral, political, and military domination, they returned from the war ready to envision and create a new world.

This was the global context in which a million African-American men and women served their country's antiracist, pro-democracy world mission—going to the battlefronts of freedom in racially segregated military forces. In such a setting it was not surprising to read in a black newspaper in 1940 the angry words, "Our war is not against Hitler in Europe . . . but against the Hitlers in America." After the Japanese attack on Pearl Harbor had led the United States to declare war against that nation and the rest of the Axis powers, a joke circulated among black draftees: "Here lies a black man killed fighting a yellow man for the glory of a white man."

It was this spirit of resistance that led the National Association for the Advancement of Colored People (NAACP) and other African-American organizations to announce early in the war their determination to carry on what they called a "Double V" campaign. This meant that black people were fighting not only for victory over racism and for freedom in Europe and Asia but also for victory against racism, segregation, and all barriers to true freedom and democracy at home in the United States.

African Americans and their leaders had surged beyond the compromise position held by W. E. B. Du Bois in 1917 at the outset of America's entry into World War I. At that point the black leader had urged his people to "forget our special grievances and close our ranks shoulder to shoulder with our own white citizens and the allied nations that are fighting for democracy." Now, in the 1940s, black Americans refused to define their grievances as "special." Instead this seemed just the moment to unequivocally call attention to the great shortcomings of democracy at home and to work for the changes that would improve every American's life.

Prior to the war, many Southern blacks had migrated North, hoping to escape the most brutal forms of racism. And even as they responded to the government's call for workers in the rapidly expanding war industries, they continued to experience discrimination in these urban areas. Everywhere they turned, black workers found that the industries that were being called "the arsenal of democracy" either had no place for them or would place them only in the lowest, dirtiest jobs, segregated from whites. Their families faced equally harsh rebuffs in their searches for homes and schools.

For large numbers of black people the war years brought an even deeper level of insult and contradiction, stemming from the awareness that blacks who served in the armed forces faced insult and abuse. Soldiers and sailors were targets of attacks by white supremacists. The U.S. Marines were unwilling to accept black men, and the Air Force was very unenthusi-

The Negro Seabees practice landing drills in 1942. More than 1 million black servicemen and -women served their country in segregated units while fighting Nazi Germany.

astic about its African-American volunteers. Although the War Department announced in 1940 that blacks would be trained as pilots, they received their training in Tuskegee, Alabama, separately from whites.

Most of the nation's military bases were in the South, and black servicemen there were subject to racial harassment, discrimination, and physical attacks on and off their bases. Several commanding officers forbade the reading of black newspapers, and when found, the papers were often confiscated and burned. At many camps, black soldiers were permitted to board buses only after white soldiers had boarded. Theaters and other entertainment facilities were segregated; at Freeman Field, Indiana, more than 100 black officers were arrested for trying to enter a white officers' club.

But black Americans were most appalled by the rapidly circulating stories about the treatment of black soldiers who were assigned to guard German prisoners of war in the United States. As they escorted their prisoners to prison camps, the black soldiers had to stand by and watch their white "enemies" being served meals on trains or in restaurants while they, the defenders of democracy, were refused service because of their race.

The anger, indignation, and determination that such experiences sparked in black communities were focused early in 1941 by A. Philip

Randolph, the head of the respected Brotherhood of Sleeping Car Porters. This eloquent fighter for justice and equality began calling for a March on Washington (MOW) to focus attention on the problem of discrimination in various industries (especially those that would be crucial when the nation went to war) and the disgraceful treatment of the black soldiers, both painful symbols of all the racial injustices harshly embedded in American life. Specifically, Randolph called for a federally sponsored Fair Employment Practices Commission (FEPC) to ensure government enforcement of desegregated employment in the war industries.

In cities across the country black people enthusiastically participated in mass meetings to organize the March on Washington. As Randolph and his national network of organizers projected it, the march would be an all-black, militant, nonviolent stand for democracy. It was scheduled to take place in the early summer. By the spring of 1941 there was so much MOW momentum in the nation's black communities that President Franklin D. Roosevelt agreed to meet with Randolph and several other black leaders of this unprecedented and unpredictable movement.

The President's major concern was to avoid an internationally embarrassing confrontation that would spotlight the deep racial contradictions

A member of the 12th Armored Division stands guard over Nazi prisoners who were captured by U.S. forces in 1945.

built into American society, just when he was preparing the nation for active participation in the European war. He tried hard to get the black leaders to give up the idea for the march as a prerequisite for serious negotiations about an FEPC. But Randolph and the others knew that fervor for the march was building in African-American communities. They also knew that the nation needed the labor of its black people in any successful mobilization for war. They refused to call off the march without a concrete Presidential commitment to an FEPC. They stood fast to their threat to bring thousands of angry African Americans to Washington to protest the nation's racism. President Roosevelt finally agreed to issue an executive order establishing a federal Fair Employment Practices Commission. This body proved to be reluctant in its work, but it was a powerful symbol of victory for an aroused and organized black community.

The March on Washington never took place, but the lessons of this victory in the African-American struggle for expanded democratic rights and economic justice were not lost on black (or white) people. Especially clear was the importance of serious organizing and the need to publicly press the nation and its leadership on the contradictions between America's worldwide reputation and its internal betrayals of democracy.

The necessities of war continued to keep these issues at the forefront of American life. For instance, Detroit, a major industrial center, attracted hundreds of thousands of black and white Southerners and other workers in search of the jobs that the war had made available. There, in the summer of 1943, many of the new opportunities and contradictions exploded.

The black and white people who had broken out of the old communities of the South on the wings of war now found new social and economic opportunities in Detroit. But they brought with them old American fears, mistrust, ignorance, and violence. As a result, the city of hope and wartime prosperity erupted in a major racial upheaval that summer. Over a period of more than 30 hours blacks and whites confronted each other in a race riot. The riot began with a fistfight between one white man and one black man and escalated until hundreds of people were involved. Only the arrival of some 6,000 federal and state troops brought the hostilities to a halt.

All over the world, African-American servicemen were overcoming their fears, preparing to fight the battles for democracy on the home front. Even before their return, they were inspiring students like the interracial group that staged sit-ins at segregated restaurants in the nation's capital, carrying signs that said, "We die together . . . Let's eat together."

In June 1941, after civil rights leader A. Philip Randolph threatened a march on Washington, President Franklin D. Roosevelt issued an order banning employment discrimination in the burgeoning war industries.

EXECUTIVE ORDER

————

REAFFIRMING POLICY OF FULL PARTICIPATION IN
THE DEFENSE PROGRAM BY ALL PERSONS, REGARDLESS
OF RACE, CREED, COLOR, OR NATIONAL ORIGIN, AND
DIRECTING CERTAIN ACTION IN FURTHERANCE OF
SAID POLICY.

WHEREAS it is the policy of the United States to encourage
full participation in the national defense program by all
citizens of the United States, regardless of race, creed, color,
or national origin, in the firm belief that the democratic way
of life within the Nation can be defended successfully only with
the help and support of all groups within its borders; and

WHEREAS there is evidence that available and needed workers
have been barred from employment in industries engaged in defense
production solely because of considerations of race, creed, color,
or national origin, to the detriment of workers' morale and of
national unity:

NOW, THEREFORE, by virtue of the authority vested in me by
the Constitution and the statutes, and as a prerequisite to the
successful conduct of our national defense production effort, I
do hereby reaffirm the policy of the United States that there shall
be no discrimination in the employment of workers in defense
industries *or government* because of race, creed, color, or national origin, and
I do hereby declare that it is the duty of employers and of labor
organizations, in furtherance of said policy and of this order, to
provide for the full and equitable participation of all workers
in defense industries, without discrimination because of race, creed,
color, or national origin;

And it is hereby ordered as follows:

1. All departments and agencies of the Government of the
United States concerned with vocational and training programs for
defense production shall take special measures appropriate to assure
that such programs are administered without discrimination because
of race, creed, color, or national origin;

In memory of
NEGRO
War Dead

CHAPTER 1

PIONEERS AND VETERANS, 1945–1950

Near the end of World War II, Adam Clayton Powell, Jr., one of black America's most internationally conscious spokesmen, tried to place the ongoing African-American freedom movement into the context of the anticolonial struggles that were rising explosively out of the discontent of the nonwhite world. Already, movements for independence had begun in British colonies in West Africa and French colonies in West and Equatorial Africa. Later, colonies in North Africa and British East Africa joined the freedom struggle. Powell, who was both a flamboyant and effective congressman from Harlem and the pastor of that community's best-known Christian congregation, the Abyssinian Baptist Church, declared:

> The black man continues on his way. He plods wearily no longer—he is striding freedom road with the knowledge that if he hasn't got the world in a jug, at least he has the stopper in his hand. . . . He is ready to throw himself into the struggle to make the dream of America become flesh and blood, bread and butter, freedom and equality. He walks conscious of the fact that he is no longer alone—no longer a minority.

Although they might not have been able to express it in Powell's colorful language, many black Americans were quite aware of the changes taking place. There were glaring differences, for instance, between where they grew up in the South and the Northern cities where they were trying to establish themselves for the first time. When they remembered the lives they had lived in places like Greenwood, Mississippi; Selma, Alabama; Shreveport, Louisiana; and dozens of smaller towns and rural areas all over the South, and then looked around them at the bright, fast-moving cities like New York, Chicago, Detroit, Philadelphia, and Gary, Indiana, how could they miss the change in those postwar years?

In 1950 a crowd gathers in Philadelphia to honor blacks who died in World War II.

17

What the newcomers soon discovered, however, was that their long strides on "freedom road" had brought them to promised lands that were filled with both positive and negative experiences. Now there was precious breathing space, releasing many of the travelers from the dangerous scrutiny of those local white Southerners who still considered black people their collective property. As they looked around and caught the sights and smells of a city like Chicago, it was obvious that the migrants had moved into the midst of the burgeoning industrial North, where they could find more jobs and better wages than they had ever dreamed of. There were schools for their children, schools whose schedules would no longer be determined by white landowners' need for agricultural workers.

Most of the new arrivals realized that the North was not heaven, but they believed that it was a place where they could escape some of the most hellish aspects of their life in the South. For instance, they did not expect ever again to have to see the bodies of men hanging from trees after they had been riddled with bullets and often mutilated. They did not expect that women would be vulnerable to rape and exploitation simply because they were black and defenseless. In the Northern cities they did not expect to have to teach their children to move out of the path when white people were approaching.

Blacks also migrated to the West and settled in cities such as Los Angeles and Seattle. One of the most exciting gifts that these new locales offered was the opportunity for black people to vote as free men and free women for the first time in their lives. Registering to vote in Philadelphia, Detroit, or Oakland did not mean risking your life and the lives of your family, risking your job or your home. In those postwar years, black people took significant advantage of this new freedom and became voters in even larger proportions than white Southerners who had migrated North. As a result, black voters in some Northern cities like Chicago and New York held the balance of power in close municipal elections.

This new political involvement brought with it another change. In most of the Northern cities where the black Southerners settled, the political structures were largely dominated by the Democratic party. Generally, the men who controlled these tightly organized political machines were eager to add the newly arrived black people to their voting tallies—as long as they thought they could control their votes. And, in fact, millions of African Americans eventually broke away from their generations-long allegiance to the Republican party—the party of Lincoln, the Great

In 1944, Harlem pastor and civil rights activist Adam Clayton Powell, Jr., became the first black person from New York City to be elected to the U.S. Congress, beginning a 26-year career in public service.

18

Although Harlem had once been a thriving center for black entrepreneurs, activists, and artists, by the 1950s, the area had declined.

Emancipator. Ironically enough, this transfer of allegiance meant that Northern blacks were now aligned with the same Democratic party that had long been dominated on the national scene by the white racist sons of the slaveholders, men who kept their control of the party largely through terrorist acts to deny black voting rights in the South. In the North, black voters were now part of that Democratic party structure and were in a position to begin to challenge its worst traditions.

Despite such rewards as finding better jobs and educational opportunities, and gaining the right to vote, this liberating movement into the Northern cities carried some clear penalties. Racism lived in many white urban neighborhoods and postwar suburbs. The rising black middle class, anxious to buy property in a "nice" neighborhood with good schools and efficient services, often bumped up against a threatening white mob and its racist rhetoric. Sometimes white resistance to black neighbors turned deadly. In Chicago, Los Angeles, Detroit, and several other cities (in both the North and the South), newly purchased homes were burned, vandalized, or had crosses burned on their lawns—a common tactic adopted by white supremacist organizations, notably the Ku Klux Klan. In one especially absurd case, when black attorney and NAACP activist George Leighton tried to move into a house in the predominantly white community of Cicero, Illinois, he was arrested for "conspiracy to lower property values."

Black citizens in Maryland register to vote in 1942. But it was another two years before black people could vote in primary elections, and two decades of costly struggle before a Voting Rights Act would guarantee those rights.

Of course, there were real estate agents and white residents who insisted that their form of segregation was not racist but driven by economic realities. They claimed to have nothing against black people but were simply worried about their homes declining in value. Sadly, their arguments were tacitly backed by the federal government—notably the Federal Housing Authority (FHA), the agency that insured homeowners' loans to low-income Americans and set housing standards. Indeed, after World War II, the FHA refused to provide mortgages to blacks moving into white neighborhoods and claimed that African Americans were regarded as poor risks for loans. The FHA also claimed that the future value of homes owned by blacks was uncertain.

Most of the new migrants could not afford to buy homes immediately, especially in the sprawling suburbs. No matter where they ended up, however—primarily the inner areas of urban centers like Chicago and Detroit—they sought to create the rich sense of community they had left behind. For even in the midst of harsh white oppression and poverty, black people, nurtured by their extended families and by their churches, had managed to build astonishing reservoirs of love, faith, and hope in the South. Such support was not readily available in the North.

Reflecting on his own Harlem childhood in *Nobody Knows My Name* (1961), the writer James Baldwin caught some of the perplexing dilemma of a city block in the long-anticipated "Promised Land" of the North.

INVISIBLE MAN

Ralph Ellison

RANDOM HOUSE *New York*

Winner of the National Book Award, Ellison's extraordinary 1952 novel explores the black quest for freedom and identity as it is expressed in the life of a young Southern-born college student who goes north to Harlem—and to many surprises—during the 1930s.

They work in the white man's world all day and come home in the evening to this fetid block. They struggle to instill in their children some private sense of honor or dignity which will help the child to survive. This means, of course, that they must struggle, stolidly, incessantly, to keep this sense alive in themselves, in spite of the insults, the indifference, and the cruelty they are certain to encounter in their working day. They patiently browbeat the landlord into fixing the heat, the plaster, the plumbing; this demands prodigious patience, nor is patience usually enough. . . . Such frustration so long endured, is driving many strong, admirable men and women whose only crime is color to the very gates of paranoia. . . .

It required the sensitivity and skills of gifted artists to capture the complexities of the changes that millions of black women, men and children were experiencing in their movement North. Baldwin was only one of the writers who tried to explain that complexity to the world. Ann Petry provided a painfully honest account of a young woman's encounter with the Northern urban reality in her novel *The Street*. Ralph Ellison's classic novel *Invisible Man* reflected the humor, anger, hope, and search for new beginnings that the urban experience represented for the transplanted black Southerners. Ellison's protagonist discovers a major difference between the South and the North when he first arrives in Harlem and begins to mingle with the evening crowds who have gathered to listen to the street-corner teachers and lecturers. Most of the rousing speeches eventually turn to the injustices of white people against people of color at home and abroad, and the young man in the novel, who has come North from Alabama, says, "I never saw so many Negroes angry in public before."

The expanding ability to be angry in public was a major part of the change that black people found in the North. In his novels, short stories, and essays, Richard Wright, the political activist and writer who had originally gone to Chicago from Mississippi in the 1920s, expressed this anger and its consequences more vividly and consistently than anyone else in his novel *Native Son* (1940).

Still, there were emotions and experiences that could never be captured by the written word. The music surging out of black communities became a powerful vehicle for communicating these feelings. The blues that had come up with the solitary old guitars from Memphis and the Mississippi Delta took on the new electricity and complexity of the cities, eventually becoming the music of small combos and big bands, pressing on toward what would soon be known as rhythm and blues. At the same time, out of the familiar settings of classic African-American jazz, piercing new sounds began to break through, offering unexpected, unresolved, and often jagged tonal edges in place of the smoother flows of the music from which it sprang. This was called "bebop" or "bop" for short. The names of its practitioners—Thelonious Monk, Dizzy Gillespie, Charlie ("Yardbird") Parker, and the young Miles Davis—and the boldness of their life-styles soon became as well known in the black community and among white jazz fans as their predecessors Lester Young, Louis Armstrong, and Coleman Hawkins.

Whatever else bop was, it was the music of change. Everything in it sounded protest, marked a determination to break out of the older, predictable harmonies. Based in places like Minton's Playhouse in Harlem, the 52nd Street jazz strip further downtown in New York City, and Los Angeles's famed Central Avenue, the irrepressible music grew out of the urgency of a postwar generation to sing its new songs, to wail and scream when necessary.

Nowhere were the songs more important than in the thousands of black churches in the Northern cities. Following the lead of vibrant women vocalists such as Mahalia Jackson, Sallie and Roberta Martin, and Sister Rosetta Tharpe, supplied with a stream of songs by the prolific gospel song-writer Rev. Thomas A. Dorsey, the churches were filled with resounding,

Charlie ("Bird") Parker, Dizzy Gillespie, and John Coltrane were among the originators of modern jazz.

rhythmic witness to the new time, as gospel singers shouted, "There's been a great change since I been born."

In the decade following World War II, more than 60 percent of the black population was still living in the South, however. And the nation's attention focused on that region as the African-American community won a series of significant battles in the courts and at the executive level of the federal government. In 1946, for example, the Supreme Court ruled that segregation on buses was unconstitutional. Two years later, the Court outlawed the use of "restrictive covenants"—codicils added on to a deed to limit the sale of a home to specific racial groups. Restrictive covenants were generally used to keep African Americans from buying homes in all-white neighborhoods. Although these gains were long overdue, they were partial outgrowths of national and international circumstances that forced President Harry S. Truman and the Democrats to pay attention to blacks.

First, Truman, his cabinet, and Congress were all concerned about America's image abroad, especially now that the United States was competing with the Soviet Union for influence over the new nations in Asia and Africa, for example, created by the collapse of European colonialism. They could not promote their version of democracy abroad as long as the United States treated its own black citizens so badly. Second, Truman's reelection in 1948 depended on black votes more than ever. This time around, the Democratic party was in utter disarray. On one side stood former Vice President Henry Wallace, who decided to run for President as a member of the newly formed Progressive party. Wallace was highly regarded in the black community; his civil rights record was impeccable, and he sought to bring the cold war with the Soviet Union to an end through cooperation rather than military threats.

On the other side were the Southern Democrats led by South Carolina senator Strom Thurmond. Their break from the Democrats further divided the vote, creating a situation in which black voters would have a decisive role in the elections. Calling themselves the States' Rights party (also known as the Dixiecrats), these Southern Democrats believed Truman's civil rights agenda had gone too far.

Because Truman had to respond to African-American and international pressure, he and his cabinet contributed to the Southern white flight from the Democratic party. The main catalyst was Truman's decision to create the first Civil Rights Commission. The commission's report, *To Secure These Rights* (1947), proposed some specific ways in which the federal government might respond to the demands of the postwar black community. For example, the report called for the establishment of a permanent federal civil rights commission—a bold and progressive proposal in those days. The report urged an end to segregation in the U.S. armed forces and pressed for laws to protect the voting rights of black people.

To Secure These Rights provided solid evidence to black people that their needs were finally being dealt with at the highest level of U.S. political life. Meanwhile, almost every year in the crucial postwar decade seemed to produce new, affirming responses from the federal courts to the dozens of challenges to segregation and disenfranchisement that the NAACP and thousands of black plaintiffs were pressing in the courts.

One of the most important of these cases, *Morgan* v. *Virginia,* was heard by the U.S. Supreme Court in 1946. Irene Morgan had firmly refused to move to the back of a Virginia-to-Baltimore Greyhound bus, as Virginia law required. She was convicted of a misdemeanor. The Court declared that the practice of segregated seating in interstate public transportation was unconstitutional and that black people traveling across state lines could not be legally forced into segregated rear seats when they arrived in a Southern state. The "back of the bus" experience was one of the most humiliating and widely known manifestations of legalized white supremacy, so word of the decision was welcomed in the nation's black communities. Irene Morgan became a hero among black Americans. But a Supreme Court decision did not guarantee change. Neither the bus companies nor the Southern states leaped to comply with the ruling. So others had to take up Irene Morgan's initiative and move it forward.

That was precisely what happened in the spring of 1947 when a group of 16 men, evenly divided between black and white, began what they called a Journey of Reconciliation. The trip was organized by a Chicago-based interracial organization known as the Congress of Racial Equality, or CORE. A relatively new offshoot from the Fellowship of Reconciliation (FOR)—a Christian pacifist organization, founded during World War I, that advocated nonviolent social change through civil disobedience—CORE was deeply committed to nonviolent direct action. Its members took inspiration from the spirit of the Indian nationalist leader Mahatma Gandhi in their quest for racial justice and reconciliation. At the same time, with the black members of the team sitting in front and the whites in back of the two Greyhound and Trailways buses that they rode from Washington, D.C., to stops in Virginia, North Carolina, and Kentucky, they were testing compli-

Under pressure from black activists, President Harry S. Truman created a Committee on Civil Rights in 1946. Two years later, he issued an executive order banning discrimination in the armed forces.

ance with the recent *Morgan* decision and urging federal enforcement of the ruling. The major immediate result of the journey was that some other black passengers felt encouraged to move toward the front of the buses. In one incident during the 15-city trip through the South, three members of the CORE team were arrested and sentenced to 21 days of hard labor on a North Carolina prison farm. The Journey of Reconciliation provided the model for the later Freedom Rides in 1961.

It took almost two decades and significant bloodshed finally to break the humiliating grip of Jim Crow—as segregation laws were called, after a character in 19th-century minstrel show that mocked blacks. Initial courtroom victories were crucial to the sense of change in black America.

Probably no legal victory of the immediate postwar years could match the overall significance of the 1944 Supreme Court decision in *Smith* v. *Allwright*. This decision essentially destroyed one of the major legal obstacles to black political participation in the South—the white primaries of the Democratic party.

Earlier in the 20th century, having claimed that their party primary voting process was the activity of private associations, Democrats managed to exclude African Americans from participating in this "private" activity. As a result, black citizens were left with little voice in government, since the Southern Democratic primaries often determined the outcome of the

Although in 1946 the Supreme Court had outlawed segregation in buses that crossed state lines, for another decade cities throughout the South would continue to enforce Jim Crow laws that required blacks to sit in the backs of buses.

general elections. African Americans refused to accept this situation, and in state after state they brought lawsuits challenging these exclusively white primaries.

In July 1940, Lonnie Smith, an African-American resident of Harris County, Texas, was stopped from voting in the Democratic party's primary election. Though he met all the legal requirements to vote, Smith was forbidden to vote because of his race. With the assistance of an NAACP legal team that included attorney Thurgood Marshall,

Smith sued election judge Allwright. Finally, in *Smith* v. *Allwright,* the Supreme Court responded to the black challengers with a judgment out-lawing the white primary process. When that happened, everyone knew that a new era was beginning: blacks across the South took that decision regarding the Texas primary as a signal to expand and intensify their voter registration activity.

With the help of a ruling by a South Carolina federal judge, J. Waties Waring, black plaintiffs won a crucial victory in that state. When South Carolina attempted to circumvent the *Smith* v. *Allwright* decision by removing all statutes relating to primaries—on the assumption that without state involvement, the Democratic primaries would be a private matter— George Elmore challenged the state's move. In the case of *Rice* v. *Elmore* (1947), Waring ruled that as long as the Democratic primary constituted the only real election in the state, blacks were entitled to participate in it.

In many places this was a dangerous resolve to take, especially in the rural South's "Black Belt"—a line of counties stretching from North Carolina to Texas, where the flat and fertile land had been dominated by cotton plantations. There, the legacy of plantation-based slavery had creat-ed counties where black people outnumbered whites in proportions of three-, four- and five-to-one—sometimes more. The obvious implications of this human arithmetic were clearly stated by one distressed white cotton gin owner. Speaking to a *New York Times* reporter, he tried to imagine what would happen if black people gained full access to the ballot box in his Tennessee county: "The niggers would take over the county if they could vote in full numbers. They'd stick together and vote blacks into every office in the county. Why you'd have a nigger judge, nigger sheriff, a nigger tax assessor—think what the black SOB's would do to you."

Ever since the days of slavery such fears were common to many white Southerners who wondered what black people would do if the racial tables were turned. Many whites found it easy to rally around the virulently racist rhetoric of a politician like Theodore G. Bilbo, U.S. senator from Missis-sippi. He voiced the fears of many Southern whites, especially the poorer ones, when he declared that World War II "and all of its great victories will not in any way or in any manner change the views and sentiments of white America on the question of social equality . . . of the negro and white race."

In a time when so much was changing, Bilbo and his fellow white supremacists were seeking guarantees that they would continue to domi-nate, and in his speeches across his state he said what so many white peo-

Senator Theodore G. Bilbo of Mississippi called on white Americans to resist the efforts of blacks to win voting rights.

plc wanted to hear. Addressing a group of county registrars during his 1946 election campaign, the first postwar campaign, and the first in which they would have to deal with black men who had risked their lives overseas for democracy, Bilbo said, "You know and I know what's the best way to keep the nigger from voting. You do it the night before the election. I don't have to tell you any more than that. Red-blooded men know what I mean."

Bilbo, however, did not have to call on white mobs to intimidate voters. Terrorist organizations such as the Ku Klux Klan and the Knights of the White Camelia, both established in 1866 immediately after the Civil War, used violence to keep African Americans from the polls as soon as the 15th Amendment was ratified in 1870. It guaranteed all men the right to vote, regardless of color. The tactics of these groups varied. Dressed in white hooded outfits, they rode through black neighborhoods; burned crosses and set fire to churches or homes; subjected blacks, Jews, Catholics, and even white women they thought were immoral to whippings; and occasionally engaged in outright assassination. Besides organizing lynch mobs, Klan members in the late 19th century targeted black Republican politicians.

Although groups such as the Klan played a major role in keeping African Americans from the polls, Southern elected officials backed by the U.S. Supreme Court were the real force. Beginning in 1890, Mississippi amended its state constitution to effectively disenfranchise black people. Between 1895 and 1903, most of the South followed suit, including South Carolina, North Carolina, Louisiana, and Alabama. Because of a poll tax imposed on the electorate, most black voters and some poor whites could not go to the polls. After 1896 all Southern states introduced "white primaries," adding another barrier to black enfranchisement. Furthermore, while literacy and property requirements were implemented, white voters were able to avoid such requirements through the use of "grandfather clauses." These turn-of-the-century clauses allowed any adult male to vote if he was the direct descendant of someone who voted in 1860. Because slavery was still in effect in 1860, the clause was intended to protect illiterate white voters. All of these measures were upheld as legal by the Supreme Court. Still, Southern states relied on illegal tactics when necessary. For example, most (but not all) well-off, literate black voters were kept from the polls by registrars who often asked potential registrants to recite the state constitution from memory to prove they were qualified to vote.

Throughout the South, white supremacists were desperate to preserve an old world that was coming to an end. They had no intention of giving up their control of the region and would use all legal means of undermining the constitutional defenses that black people increasingly depended on. Many also conspired to use illegal means, from economic coercion to acts of terrorism, to keep their black fellow Southerners "in their place."

Nowhere was this new world more evident than in the ranks of the thousands of African Americans who returned from the battlegrounds of World War II. They were the ones who seemed most ready to demonstrate the truth of Adam Clayton Powell's statement that black people were "ready to throw [themselves] into the struggle to make the dream of America become flesh and blood." A recently discharged army corporal from Alabama spoke for many of his black comrades in 1945 when he declared, "I spent four years in the army to free a bunch of Dutchmen and Frenchmen, and I'm hanged if I'm going to let the Alabama version of the Germans kick me around when I get home. No sirree-bob! I went into the Army a nigger; I'm comin' out a man."

Among those determined to win voting rights for blacks in the South was a solid core of veterans who felt like they had earned the right to vote after risking their lives for democracy overseas. In 1946, for instance, Isaac Newton returned home from the war to Wrightsville, Georgia, and he was determined to vote even though neighbors warned him not to. When he went to register, he was shot dead. In Mississippi that same year brothers Charles and Medgar Evers came home from the war to their town of Decatur, determined to vote. When they arrived at the registrar's office, a group of armed white neighbors blocked their way. One of them snarled, "Who you niggers think you are?" Medgar replied, "We've grown up here. We have fought for this country and we should register." But they were driven away from the registrar's desk,

Returning black World War II veterans began the job search at home with renewed determination to live and work as "first-class citizens" of America.

On April 18, 1947, the world took note as Jackie Robinson hit the first home run of his career with the Brooklyn Dodgers, 10 days after becoming the first black player to break the segregation of major league baseball.

and one of the white men predicted that there would be "trouble" if these black citizens persisted in their attempts to register and vote. But he could never have guessed the nature of the coming trouble. For the Evers brothers and thousands like them would return all over the South to challenge the keepers of the old terror.

The powerful thrusts of postwar change were not confined to politics. A remarkable change in the world of sports captured the attention of the rest of the nation. Jackie Robinson, another veteran of the war and a baseball player with the Kansas City Monarchs of the segregated Negro Leagues, was signed by the Brooklyn Dodgers in 1945. The action broke the 20th century–long racial barrier in major league baseball, the "national pastime." An outstanding athlete who had lettered in baseball, basketball, track, and football at the University of California at Los Angeles, an outspoken critic of America's racial betrayals of democracy, the 28-year-old Robinson spent a year with the Dodgers' farm team in Montreal before finally joining the Brooklyn lineup in the spring of 1947. Black people were ecstatic.

Meanwhile, Robinson made his way through the minefields of the Southern towns and cities where spring training was held in those days—

rigidly segregated places where the feeding and housing of a black man presented a major challenge. No one could predict, but many sensed, the extraordinary future of black athletes in the United States by the time Robinson won the National League's Most Valuable Player award in 1949.

The black community followed local and national developments in civil rights by reading African American newspapers such as the *Pittsburgh Courier*, the *Chicago Defender*, the *Baltimore Afro-American*, and the *Norfolk Journal and Guide*. These papers were circulated through many hands in households, barbershops, beauty parlors, churches, and restaurants. In the hands of Pullman car porters, the black sleeping car attendants on intercity trains, they found their way into the Deep South as well.

By reading boldly presented news stories and columns, black people followed the anticolonial, independence-oriented exploits of the darker-skinned majority of the world in places like India, Africa, and China. There were constant references to Gandhi, who had spent decades challenging his people in India to wage a nonviolent struggle for independence against the great British empire that governed them. Repeatedly, the black newspapers carried letters and editorials contending that Gandhi's movement offered a model for black America, especially in the South. Mordecai Johnson, president of Howard University in Washington, D.C.; Howard Thurman, mystically oriented preacher and dean of Howard University's chapel; and Benjamin Mays, president of Morehouse College in Atlanta, were some of the best known black Americans who had made the pilgrimage to the ashrams, the humble communal villages where Gandhi based himself. Invariably, Gandhi met his African-American visitors with sincere openness to the possibility that black Americans might become a shining second generation in the experimental nonviolent struggles for liberation.

Gandhi's life and teaching mirrored some of the best African-American traditions. Like the 19th-century abolitionists David Walker and Frederick Douglass, like W. E. B. Du Bois, the antilynching activist and newspaperwoman Ida B. Wells-Barnett, and Howard Thurman, Gandhi believed that the despised of the earth actually carried within their own lives and history the seeds of healing transformation for themselves, their oppressors, and their world. So when black Americans identified their struggle as part of a larger, worldwide movement, it was not simply the idea "that [we are] no longer alone" that compelled them. It was also the vision that as the rising children of their enslaved forbears, they—like Gandhi's masses—might have some liberating gift to offer to the world.

A powerful, passionate orator, Paul Robeson used his influence to speak out about the plight of African Americans and other persecuted peoples.

While blacks were developing an understanding of worldwide repression, the U.S. government seemed to be, in some instances, supporting that repression. On the one hand, U.S. foreign policy appeared to link the United States with the interests and points of view of its white, Western allies, such as England, France, Portugal, and white South Africa, countries still deeply identified with colonial domination. On the other hand, as part of the deepening cold war against the Soviet Union, the United States was also projecting itself as "the leader of the free world," avowedly concerned for the rights of oppressed people everywhere, especially people of color who might be tempted to turn to the Soviet Union and to other socialist and communist movements for assistance in their freedom struggles.

So when black leaders with socialist sympathies, such as W. E. B. Du Bois and the politically active actor, singer, and scholar Paul Robeson, spoke out on behalf of the nonwhite peoples and their freedom struggles, when they articulated too positive a view of the Russian Revolution's social and economic ambitions, when they sharply criticized U. S. foreign and domestic policy, the U.S. government considered them un-American and dangerous. The passports of both men were confiscated to prevent them from traveling and speaking abroad on behalf of the anticolonial movements and against the reign of white supremacy in America. Still, both men continued to speak out. But the price they paid was very high. Robeson essentially lost his lucrative concert career, and ultimately his health. Du Bois, in the fearful climate of anticommunism in America, found himself deserted by many people who had benefited from his decades of unstinting service to the cause of freedom, justice, and democratic hope, and he moved permanently to Africa.

Anticommunist fervor virtually crushed these two intellectual giants, but it could not crush the movement. In the streets and in the courts, black activists forced the federal government to admit that segregation was wrong and must be remedied. By 1954, it became evident to all that African Americans, like their counterparts in the colonial world, would no longer wait for the birth of a new freedom.

Black students and their families in Prince Edward County, Virginia, were among the plaintiffs in the NAACP's challenge to school segregation.

CHAPTER 2

JIM CROW MUST GO!: THE ROAD FROM BROWN TO MONTGOMERY

◇ ◇ ◇

Revolutions always exact a price from their participants. People have lost their livelihoods, lost friends and family, lost their connection to community, even lost their lives. The movement to end segregation and press America to live up to its creed of justice for all was no different. Nowhere was this personal cost more obvious than in the five legal cases that would force their way into the U.S. Supreme Court and become known collectively as *Brown* v. *Board of Education*. The case known as *Briggs* v. *Elliott* provided the legal bedrock on which the entire set of *Brown* cases was built.

The setting for this initial drama was in many ways an unlikely situation for protest. Clarendon County, South Carolina, was known for its bitter resistance to any attempts at changing the brutal traditions of white supremacy. It was a people's love for their children that drove them to take the simple but dangerous risk of confronting the school board with their children's need for bus transportation to their segregated school. The white children had several buses, while the black children, who outnumbered the others, had no buses at all. Of course, the black parents and their supporters were also aware that the all-white school board spent more money on each white child in the county than on each black one. They knew this to be the general pattern throughout the South. What the adults had to figure out was how to deal with the rude and repeated rebuffs from the school board and its chairman, R. W. Elliott, who said at a meeting with black people, "We ain't got no money to buy a bus for your nigger children."

Then Rev. J. A. Delaine, a local black pastor and school superintendent in Summerton, met Rev. James A. Hinton, a regional representative for the NAACP, at a meeting at Allen College. Allen was one of the black colleges in Columbia, about 60 miles from Summerton. Hinton told the

33

gathering that the NAACP was trying to find men and women to become plaintiffs in a case that would challenge the legality of the segregated schools, beginning with the fact that none of the black schoolchildren were supplied with buses. Delaine knew after the meeting that he had to become the bridge between the unrelenting but frustrated neighbor parents and the national organization.

Several parents accepted the risks and sued the school board. One of the plaintiffs, Liza Briggs, worked as a maid for a local motel, and she was told by her employer to choose between her job or the lawsuit. She chose to remain a plaintiff, because giving up her role in the case, she said, "would be hurting the children." So she lost the job and gained a future.

Delaine and his wife worked for the school board they were suing, and both lost their jobs. They also lost their home and their church when the buildings were burned to the ground. Meanwhile, in Farmville, Virginia, in 1951, a courageous 16-year-old high school junior organized her fellow students to fight for equal facilities for black schools. Under Barbara Rose Johns's dynamic leadership, the black students at the woefully inadequate Moton High not only went on strike but arranged with the NAACP to file a desegregation lawsuit in their county. That suit was eventually tied to the one initiated by Oliver Brown of Topeka, Kansas, on

The Supreme Court, in Brown v. Board of Education, *ruled that segregated black schools like this one were inherently unequal.*

Attorneys George E. C. Hayes, Thurgood Marshall, and James M. Nabrit share congratulations as they leave the U.S. Supreme Court building on May 17, 1954, the day school segregation in the United States was officially outlawed by the Court's decision in Brown v. Board of Education.

behalf of his daughter Linda and all the black children of their city.

The Topeka school board had denied Linda Brown admission to a school just five blocks from her home, forcing her to make a long commute across town, because her neighborhood school was for whites only. Charles Houston and Thurgood Marshall of the NAACP Legal Defense and Education Fund were the attorneys for the Browns. In his Supreme Court argument, Marshall presented evidence that separating black and white students placed the blacks at a great disadvantage. Marshall's strategy was to force the Supreme Court to overturn *Plessy* v. *Ferguson*, the 1896 ruling upholding the legality of segregation as long as states provided "separate but equal" facilities to African Americans. Such practices, he said, violated the 14th Amendment to the Constitution, which guarantees equal protection of the laws. Once he was able to get the Court to overturn *Plessy*, Marshall did not have to prove that facilities set aside for "colored only" were unequal to those set aside for whites. To buttress his argument, Marshall brought in pioneering black psychologists Mamie and Kenneth Clark, whose research demonstrated that African-American children in inferior, segregated schools had a negative self-image and generally performed poorly as a result.

When the Supreme Court handed down its unanimous decision in *Brown* on Monday, May 17, 1954, it was a stunning accomplishment. All eyes focused on the solemn announcement that "in the field of public education the doctrine of 'separate but equal' has no place." After more than half a century of determined struggle, black people and their allies had finally turned the Supreme Court around, leading it to abandon *Plessy* v. *Ferguson.* Two days after *Brown,* the *Washington Post* declared, "It is not too much to speak of the court's decision as a new birth of freedom." On a more personal level, many black people shared the reaction of Robert Williams, a young North Carolinian who was in the U.S. Marine Corps at the time, who recalled in his memoirs:

> My inner emotions must have been approximate to the Negro slaves' when they first heard about the Emancipation Proclamation. Elation took hold of me so strongly that I found it very difficult to refrain from yielding to an urge of jubilation . . . On this momentous night of May 17, 1954, I felt that at last the government was willing to assert itself on behalf of first-class citizenship, even for Negroes. I experienced a sense of loyalty that I had never felt before. I was sure that this was the beginning of a new era of American democracy.

Perhaps it was only the vital opening of a new chapter in the long black struggle for authentic democracy in America. But it forced individual men and women to make hard, exciting choices about how they would lead their own lives. In Boston, Martin Luther King, Jr., and his new bride, the former Coretta Scott, had been facing such choices together ever since their marriage in June 1953, and his completion of the coursework for his doctorate in theology at Boston University. Soon Coretta would complete her three years of work in music education at the New England Conservatory of Music, and the choices they had been wrestling with were now leading to a move from Boston to Montgomery, Alabama.

Born in Atlanta in January 1929, Martin was the beloved first son of Martin Luther King, Sr., one of that city's leading Baptist ministers, and his wife, Alberta Williams King, whose father had been the founding pastor of Ebenezer Baptist Church, the congregation now headed by King Senior. The younger King entered Morehouse College in Atlanta, one of the most respected black colleges in the nation, when he was only 15. He became a popular student leader and a serious student.

*Benjamin Mays,
president of
Morehouse College
in Atlanta, was a
staunch advocate of
human rights. His
life and teachings
had a lasting impact
on Martin Luther
King, Jr.*

When he was 18, not long before he graduated from Morehouse with a B.A. in sociology, King decided to stop resisting an inner calling to the Christian ministry. So his father proudly ordained the young man who had finally decided that he would not take the path of law or medicine, possibilities that had intrigued him for a while. At that point in his life young "M.L." was often torn between the image of ministry he saw in his father— a pietistic man with an engaging, emotionally charged approach—and the one he found in Benjamin Mays, Morehouse's president. Mays's combination of profound spirituality, intellect, and commitment to social justice left a deep mark on the lives of many of his "Morehouse Men."

Martin King, Jr., left Atlanta in 1948 to enroll at Crozer Theological Seminary in Chester, Pennsylvania (one of the few white theological schools that accepted more than one or two black men in each entering class). He carried with him a profound sense of identity with the black church, community, and extended family that had done so much to shape and nurture him. Although he knew that he did not want to be the kind of preacher that his father was, King was deeply appreciative of the older man's unwavering religious faith and his readiness to confront racism.

So although Crozer was King's first extended experience in an overwhelmingly white institution, he was spiritually and mentally prepared for it. By now the young Atlantan, whose eloquence was praised by his professors, was firmly grounded in the way of thinking that marked the lives of many young black people in those days. He knew that his life and career were not simply matters of personal success and advancement. Instead, he recognized and acknowledged an inextricable connection to the "cause" of black advancement, to the responsibility he bore for fighting for "the uplift of the race." King graduated from Crozer in 1951 as valedictorian of his class and received a coveted fellowship to pursue his doctorate at Boston University. The decision to do doctoral work reflected King's continuing exploration of the possibility that he might somehow combine his love for academic work with his passion for the Christian ministry.

In Boston, King was introduced to Coretta Scott, a bright, attractive young woman who had grown up not far from Selma, Alabama. Living in the rural South of the 1930s and 1940s, Coretta saw many instances of violently enforced white domination, including the beating of her father. With these disturbing memories of the past and her own professional ambitions on her mind, Coretta King was strongly inclined to stay out of the South. And King was attracted by invitations to consider positions in the North.

Martin Luther King, Jr., third from left in the first row, was a young sociology student at Morehouse College when he decided to pursue the ministry.

But, King later remembered, "The south, after all, was our home. Despite its shortcomings we loved it as home. . . ." At the same time, Martin and Coretta King were part of the long black Southern tradition that called on its educated young people to work to change the South they had known. This was the context for King's statement that "[we] had a real desire to do something about the problems that we had felt so keenly as youngsters. We never wanted to be considered detached spectators."

So Coretta was neither very surprised nor very resistant when her husband finally declared that they were going to live in the South. By the spring of 1954 King had accepted an invitation to the pastorate of Dexter Avenue Baptist Church in Montgomery, Alabama, the city known as "The Cradle of the Confederacy." Montgomery was where Jefferson Davis had been sworn in as president of the pro-slavery states that seceded from the Union in 1861. By the time King began his official tenure as pastor of Dexter's middle-class congregation in September 1954, it was clear that the city's black population of close to 50,000 was on the brink of a new time.

Like their counterparts throughout the South, many of the most activist-oriented members of Montgomery's black population had been prodded into new forms of organizing. For instance, the expanding, state-by-state defeat of the segregated white primary system inspired the creation of a number of voter registration organizations and campaigns in Montgomery. It also encouraged a variety of risky experiments to challenge the humiliating segregation of everyday life.

One of the most important of these experiments was the formation of the Women's Political Council (WPC), a well-organized group of black, middle-class women. They developed an important telephone communications link (called a "telephone tree" in those days) among their members, initially used for voter registration campaigns. But eventually the group expanded its concerns to other issues faced by a black community in a white-dominated segregated city. In the early 1950s these issues ranged from black citizens' seeking access to the public parks that their taxes helped to maintain to the constantly vexing matter of the harsh treatment black people received on the local buses.

It was not long before King discovered that the creative and outspoken chairperson of the WPC, JoAnn Robinson, a faculty member at Alabama State College, the local black college, was a member of Dexter's congregation. He quickly recruited her to lead the church's Social and Political Action Committee, which he had organized. In turn, as Robinson and her conscientious group of women took their concerns into the chambers of the Montgomery City Council, she often called on her young pastor to go with them to add his sharp mind, eloquent voice, and passionate commitment to justice to their arguments for change.

In Montgomery, as elsewhere in the South, those black citizens demanding justice included many military veterans. The Reverend Ralph David Abernathy, pastor of First Baptist Church, was one of the best known of these veterans. He had served with the U.S. Army in Europe, then returned to study at Montgomery's Alabama State College and earn his master's degree in sociology at Atlanta University. As Abernathy later recalled of those days in Montgomery, "Many of the older clergy were in favor of sweeping social change, but they were willing for it to come about slowly, when white society was ready to accept it." But he also remembered that some of the religious leaders had less patience. "Those of us in our twenties were less patient and less afraid of making trouble. . . . As we talked with one another, we began saying that we were willing to help tear down the old walls, even if it meant a genuine uprising."

Another highly regarded veteran freedom worker who was ready for change was E. D. Nixon, the gruff-voiced, outspoken Pullman car porter who had worked for years with the legendary A. Philip Randolph organizing the Brotherhood of Sleeping Car Porters, the most influential African-American labor union in the country. Now in his 50s, Nixon was probably best known for his role as president of the Alabama branch of the NAACP and as an unrelenting campaigner for black citizenship rights, especially the right to vote. In his NAACP role, Nixon was quietly and efficiently assisted by a highly respected woman in her early 40s who served as secretary to the local NAACP branch and as adviser to the organization's youth council. A seamstress by profession, she was named Rosa Parks, and she turned out to be less patient than she sometimes seemed.

By 1955, it was not just Montgomery's black pastors, NAACP members, and community leaders who sensed with Martin and Coretta King that something remarkable was happening. Many of the city's ordinary black citizens recognized that they were entering a new time.

Of course, they (and the rest of the nation, even the world) also knew about the brutal lynching of 14-year-old Emmett Till, who was beaten and killed in Mississippi in 1955 by two white men after Till made the mistake

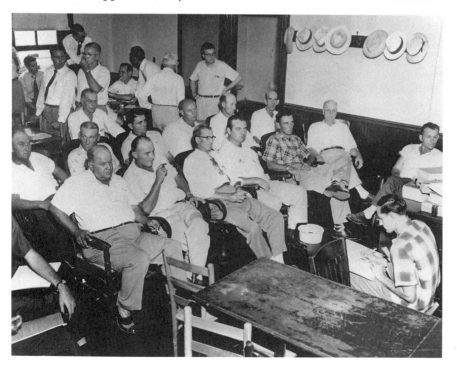

This all-white jury acquitted the men accused of killing young Emmett Till, but the murder, publicity, and the verdict invigorated advocates of racial justice nationwide.

of speaking familiarly to a white woman, the wife of one of the men. The black newspapers and journals spread the word (and the photos) of the murdered teenager whose Chicago upbringing had not prepared him for the proper approach to a white woman in rural Mississippi. The papers also reported that black congressman Charles Diggs, Jr., of Michigan, and national NAACP officials went to Money, Mississippi, to attend the trial of Till's accused killers, along with Till's mother, Mamie Till, who helped to turn the tragedy of her son's death into a rallying point for the civil rights movement. Because she insisted on an open casket, and allowed photographs, people nationwide saw firsthand the horrors of Southern lynching.

In spite of the predictable not-guilty verdict in the Till murder case that summer, the black people of Montgomery realized they had seen signals of a new time: In the heart of Bilbo's Mississippi, keepers of the past had been forced to hold a trial, to face a black member of the U.S. House of Representatives (though they tried to tighten their grip on the past by calling Congressman Diggs "boy"); they had been pressed to recognize the rising power of an inflamed black community at home and to answer hard questions from people of color and of conscience from around the world.

For many ordinary black citizens some of their most painful and consistently humiliating encounters with white power and injustice took place in public, especially on city buses. In the mid-1950s the automobile had not yet become the ubiquitous presence that it is now—especially not for the thousands of black people in Montgomery who earned their living as maids, cooks, janitors, porters, and the like. High school and college students were also part of the 17,000 or so black people who made up some 75 percent of the passengers on the segregated buses. During their daily rides, blacks were relegated to the often-crowded back area and were forbidden to take vacant seats in the forward white section, even if no white passengers were present. Beyond this were the all-too-common encounters with rude and hostile white bus drivers (there were no black ones) who often called their black passengers "apes," "niggers," "black cows," and other demeaning names. Often they demanded that blacks get up and surrender their seats to white passengers when the white section was full. Black passengers were also required to pay their fare in front and then get off to re-board through the rear door. And it was not unusual for drivers to pull away before a slower or older passenger could get to the rear door.

Such practices were common on the buses in cities all over the South, but that did not make them any more palatable. Indeed, a daily diet

Many black women in Montgomery worked as domestics, caring for the homes and children of white people. Most traveled to their jobs on buses that were still segregated in the mid-1950s.

of such injustice became more than some people could take, and various forms of resistance erupted. For instance, in the spring of 1955 a teen-aged Montgomery high school student named Claudette Colvin loudly resisted both the driver's orders to give up her seat and the police who were called to arrest her. Colvin's screams and curses were not quite what leaders like Robinson and Nixon had in mind as they searched for a case that could be used to challenge the constitutionality of Montgomery's segregated seating. Their aim was to rally the black community to experiment with a brief boycott of the buses that would focus not only on the segregated seating but on the humiliating treatment. Colvin was not the test case they needed, but Nixon and the waiting WPC forces knew that someone else would eventually be pressed beyond the limit and would resist. Evicted in the early 1940s for sitting too far forward, Rosa Parks, who had long served as a freedom worker, provided the opportunity that Nixon and the WPC needed.

On December 1, 1955, quiet, soft-spoken Rosa Parks did what she had to do. After all, she was a veteran freedom worker and in many ways one of the most prepared for this historic moment. During the previous decade, she had served as secretary of the Montgomery branch of the

NAACP, worked on voter registration campaigns, and had run the local NAACP Youth Council. Because of her earlier challenge to bus segregation ordinances, a few bus drivers refused to stop for her. Perhaps she remembered how right she had felt the previous summer at the Tennessee training center for social change called Highlander Folk School, as she talked with other black and white participants about Montgomery and what was needed there. They talked about their South and how they might contribute to the powerful transformation unfolding everywhere. Perhaps she remembered the young people of her NAACP Youth Council and the models they needed.

So when a bus driver told Parks and three other black people in her row to get up and relinquish their seats to a white man who was standing, she had to say no. There were no shouts, no curses, no accusations, just an inwardly powerful woman sensing the strength of her conviction and refusing to move. When, inevitably, policemen boarded the bus and one ordered her to get up, she still had to say no, realizing that arrest would be the next step. Rosa Parks, the magnificently proper and respectable church member, prepared to go to jail, in a time when such people did not go to such places. But first she responded to the policeman who asked her why she did not obey the driver. She said, "I didn't think I should have to." Then she asked the officer, "Why do you push us around?" His response may have been the only one he could give: "I don't know." Yet he revealed his own entrapment in the system: "But the law is the law, and you are under arrest." And he took Rosa Parks to the police station.

At the station Parks called her friend and NAACP coworker, E. D. Nixon. For the veteran freedom worker, the shock of Parks's arrest was immediately mixed with the conviction that this was the test case that would challenge the city's bus segregation laws. After informing Parks's husband, Raymond, and her mother, Nixon immediately contacted two local whites he knew he could depend on, Clifford and Virginia Durr. Clifford Durr was a white lawyer in private practice, and he and Nixon went to the station to bail out Rosa Parks. Immediately they began discussing with her the possibility that her arrest could develop into the test case they all needed, and that she needed to recognize the physical and economic risks this might entail. After some hesitation on the part of her husband, Parks and her family were ready.

But history, JoAnn Robinson, and the black people of Montgomery soon overtook those original plans. For when Robinson heard the news of Parks's adventure she realized that the arrest of her friend was potentially more powerful than a legal case. She began to use the telephone tree that her WPC had developed for its voter registration work, and soon dozens of black people knew that the highly respected Rosa Parks had been arrested for refusing to cooperate with the humiliating bus segregation practices that troubled them all. Working all that night and into the next morning, Robinson managed to compose, type the stencil, and run off more than 30,000 mimeographed copies of a leaflet that said:

> Another Negro woman has been arrested and thrown in jail because she refused to get up out of her seat on the bus for a white person to sit down. It is the second time since the Claudette Colvin case that a Negro woman has been arrested for the same thing. This has to be stopped. Negroes have rights, too, for if Negroes did not ride the buses, they could not operate. Three-fourths of the riders are Negroes, yet we are arrested, or have to stand over empty seats. If we do not do something to stop these arrests, they will continue. The next time it may be you, or your daughter, or mother. This woman's case will come up on Monday. We are, therefore, asking every Negro to stay off the buses Monday in protest of the arrest and trial. Don't ride the bus to work, to town, to school, or anywhere on Monday. You can afford to stay out of school for one day if you have no other way to go except by bus. You can also afford to stay out of town for one day. If you work, take a cab, or walk. But please, children and grown-ups, don't ride the bus at all on Monday. Please stay off all buses Monday.

That morning, Friday, December 2, with the assistance of some of her students and WPC coworkers, Robinson blanketed the black community with the leaflets. By then, Nixon had begun to mobilize the traditional black community leaders, especially the ministers. It soon became clear that both his and Robinson's best instincts had been right: there was a powerful and positive reaction to the call for the leaders to meet and respond both to Parks's arrest and to Robinson's call for a boycott.

By that evening the local community leaders, including King, had decided to confirm Robinson's initiative and agreed that the next Monday, December 5, would be the day for a one-day experimental boycott. Since that was also the day for which Parks's trial was scheduled, it seemed logical to call for a mass community meeting that evening. In order to spread the word of Monday's boycott and mass meeting, the leadership group was depending upon another leaflet, many phone calls, and crucially, the dozens of black church services scheduled for Sunday, December 4. Then, when one of the leaflets got into the hands of a white employer and was passed on to the *Montgomery Advertiser*, the city's daily newspaper, a great gift of publicity was handed to the planners: a Sunday morning front page story on the planned boycott and mass meeting.

Of course, no one could be certain how the black community would respond to the call. There was significant fear among the leaders, including King, that a combination of apathy and fear might overwhelm the sense of righteous indignation that people felt. Nor could anyone predict how white people, especially the more rigid and violence-prone segregationists, would respond. All over the South, many white men and women had been eagerly rallying to the calls of the White Citizens Council to defend segregation by any means necessary. The local Ku Klux Klan was also very much alive and well, carrying on its periodic marches and car caravans through Montgomery's black community, knowing that their reputation for lynchings, beatings, and bombings was enough to drive most blacks off the streets and porches behind the relative safety of closed doors. It was clear to blacks that there was real physical danger involved in the simple act of not riding the buses. But for a lot of black riders there might be even more economic danger if their employers objected to such black initiative and protest.

Rosa Parks, who refused to give up her bus seat to a white man in Montgomery, was accompanied by NAACP activist E. D. Nixon (second from left) as she appealed her conviction.

As a result, it was impossible to predict what the results of the boycott attempt would be. Until the earliest buses began moving in the black community to take people to work on Monday morning, the leaders of the courageous experiment felt the action would be successful if 60 percent of the riders stayed off the buses. That cold and cloudy morning, as Martin and Coretta King looked out their front window toward a nearby bus stop, the uncertain victory now seemed clear. Most of the buses moving by were empty. Neither apathy nor fear had prevailed. Then, as King went out to drive along the black community bus routes, he saw an extraordinary scene: everywhere, black people were walking, thumbing rides, walking, riding mules, walking, resurrecting old horse and buggy contraptions, taking taxis. Some older men and women were walking more than five miles each way, at times saying, "I'm walking for my grandchildren." Meanwhile, all the buses from the black communities were at least 95 percent empty.

King recognized instinctively that more than bus seating, more than painful memories of humiliation, even more than solidarity with Rosa Parks was at stake here. As he said later, "A miracle had taken place. The once dormant and quiescent Negro community was now fully awake." At the same time, King's own personal awakening, inextricably tied to the rising of the people of Montgomery, was still in process. That Monday afternoon, he gathered with 20 or so other local leaders to assess and celebrate the overwhelming success of the almost spontaneous boycott and to plan for the evening's mass meeting. King was then surprised to find himself—one of the youngest and newest community leaders—nominated and elected president of the new organization that they had just brought into being at that session, the Montgomery Improvement Association.

The immediate task of the new MIA leaders was to build on the powerful momentum of the one-day boycott. They decided to move rather slowly, to focus first on the simple need for more courteous and humane treatment of black bus riders. They also called for what Coretta King—and later others—ruefully described as "a more humane form of segregation," which would allow white riders to fill the buses from the front to the middle, black riders from back to middle, with no need for anyone to have to give up a seat. They also pressed for the hiring of black drivers in black neighborhoods. The new MIA leadership decided to call for black people to continue the boycott until these changes were made.

That night at the first mass meeting at the large Holt Street Baptist Church, the leaders immediately recognized that an extraordinary spirit was taking hold. After a day of walking and working, hundreds of Montgomery's black people began to file into the church as much as two hours before the scheduled starting time of 7:00 P.M. As they waited, filling the sanctuary with their songs and prayers, it was possible to feel the high enthusiasm that ran through the crowded benches. By 7:00, there were thousands swirling around outside, downstairs, in the main sanctuary, and up in the balcony. The crowd was so dense and animated that King and the other speakers had a hard time pushing their way to the pulpit.

After opening with the triumphant singing of "Onward, Christian Soldiers," the meeting continued with a number of what would have to be called freedom sermons, more songs and spirituals, announcements, and testimonies. One of the few white reporters on hand, Joe Azbell of the *Advertiser,* was almost awestruck by the experience he witnessed, including the consideration shown to him as a white person. The next day he wrote, "The meeting was much like an old-fashioned revival with loud applause added. . . . It proved beyond any doubt that there was a discipline among Negroes that many whites had doubted. It was almost a military discipline combined with emotion."

As the new MIA president and featured speaker, King had to decide how to position himself in the midst of the dynamic power he had recognized among the people since early in the morning. The 26-year-old pastor later described his struggle to figure out the correct approach:

> How could I make a speech that would be militant enough to keep my people aroused to positive action and yet moderate enough to keep this fervor within controllable and Christian bounds? I knew that many of the Negro people were victims of bitterness that could easily rise to flood proportions. What could I say to keep them courageous and prepared for positive action and yet devoid of hate and resentment? Could the militant and the moderate be combined in a single speech?

In what might be called a freedom sermon, combining the vivid preaching style found in the black churches with the content of the freedom movement, the young pastor set the people and their movement in their largest context that night. He identified them "first and foremost" as American citizens, citizens who had the right and the responsibility to protest injustice and to work for a better society. At every point he grounded himself in the concrete experience of Montgomery's black people and their experiences on the buses and elsewhere in their unjust, humiliating and segregated city. So there was constant enthusiastic and empathetic verbal response all through his presentation, particularly when King uttered the words, "There comes a time when people get tired of being trampled over by the iron feet of oppression." He pushed even further, pressing on the audience a sense of identity beyond their status as victims of oppression, declaring, "I want to say that we're not here advocating violence. . . . We have never done that. . . . I want it to be known throughout Montgomery and throughout this nation that we are a Christian people. . . . We believe in the Christian religion. We believe in the teachings of Jesus. The only weapon that we have in our hands this evening is the weapon of protest." All through that statement of their central religious identity the people shouted and applauded, moved with King, pressed him forward even as he urged them toward their own best possibilities. King worked hard to assure and strengthen the people, encouraging the walking community to know that "we are not wrong." Indeed, he placed them in the company of the Supreme Court, assured them that the nation's Constitution was on their side. He went on, "If we are wrong, God almighty is wrong. . . . If we are wrong, Jesus of Nazareth was merely a utopian dreamer who never came down to earth." King helped to prepare the people for the long journey that had already begun that morning. He said, "We, the disinherited of this land, we who have been oppressed so long, are tired of going through the long night of captivity. And now we are reaching out for the daybreak of freedom and justice and equality."

So the issue was already far beyond the buses, encompassing freedom, justice, and equality. Calling upon the people to continue to work together for much more than a desegregated bus seat, King set an example for the freedom movement leadership. For he declared to his community:

> Right here in Montgomery, when the history books are written in the future . . . somebody will have to say, "There lived a race of people . . . who had the moral courage to stand up for their rights. . . . And thereby they injected a new meaning into the veins of history and of civilization." And we're going to do that. God grant that we will do it before it is too late.

The excited, inspired people hardly had time to consider this grand calling to be the bearers of

Martin Luther King, Jr., with Coretta King at left, appears at the Montgomery County Courthouse in March 1956 to be tried on charges of violating the state's law against boycotts. King was one of 115 Montgomery Improvement Association leaders indicted under the law.

Carpools organized by churches and women's groups provided transportation for black workers during the 11-month-long Montgomery bus boycott.

new universal values when they were brought right back to the concrete realities of their new movement. Right there in the meeting they were called upon to vote their approval of the proposals the MIA leadership was using as a basis for their negotiating with the city administration and the bus company. They were also told that private automobiles and black-owned taxis had to be volunteered, along with drivers, for use in a car pool that would soon become the most highly organized element of the boycott movement. And, of course, money had to be collected, for gas, for maintenance, and for all the other expenses connected to the development of an essentially volunteer organization. So the marvelously ordinary black men and women who were just being called upon by King to inject "a new meaning into the veins of history and of civilization" were also being asked to drop their hard-earned quarters and dollars into the MIA collection baskets.

The sense that something new was being born in Montgomery's black churches had drawn black leaders from other parts of Alabama to the initial meeting that night. They came from such places as Birmingham, Mobile, Tuskegee, and Tuscaloosa, both to encourage the people of Montgomery and to gain new inspiration for their own struggles. Still, it is quite possible that the expansion of the boycott's inspiring potential might have simply been confined to Alabama if its white opponents had not made a series of mistakes, mistakes based on their stubborn refusal to realize that a new time and a new black community were emerging.

First, in the earliest attempts at negotiation, the representatives of the city and the bus company refused to make even the slightest accommodation to the relatively modest changes the MIA leadership was proposing. This stiff resistance on the part of the white leaders helped to steel the resolve of the aroused and walking people. Then the city commissioners inaugurated what they called a "get tough" policy with the boycotters and their leadership. Legal harassment of the crucial cabs and car pool, and an unjustified arrest of King for speeding were part of the strategy of intimidation. This was soon followed by a publicly announced decision by all three city commissioners to join the local White Citizens Council, a slightly more respectable version of the Klan.

Such actions only compelled black Montgomery to form a deeper resolve to stay off the buses. Then the most important of the early opposition mistakes took place on Monday night, January 30, 1956, almost two months into the boycott. That night, while King was at one of the mass meetings, his wife and young child were at home accompanied by a member of Dexter church. The two women heard something hit the front porch. They ran to the back room where three-month-old Yolanda Denise was sleeping. What they had heard was a stick of dynamite landing on the front porch, and its explosion blew a hole in the porch floor, shattered four windows, and damaged a porch column. Running to the back had saved Coretta King and her friend from possible injury.

Called out of the mass meeting, King arrived at his house some 15 minutes after the blast. There he found hundreds of angry black people—some of them armed—milling around his front porch. After determining that his family was safe, he came back out to address the crowd, some of whom were fiercely challenging the chief of police and the mayor to match them gun for gun, and defiantly refusing to obey police orders to disperse. "Getting tough" was obviously an approach that had epidemic possibilities, but when King appeared he maintained an extraordinary and crucial composure that transformed the situation. After assuring the crowd that his family had not been harmed, he said,

> We believe in law and order. Don't get panicky. . . . Don't get your weapons. He who lives by the sword will perish by the sword. Remember, that is what God said. We are not advocating violence. We want to love our enemies. Be good to them. Love them and let them know you love them.

After urging that stern and demanding post-dynamite discipline upon himself and the crowd, pressing them to apply the tenets of their religion to the crisis of that night, King went on to remind the quieting crowd, "I did not start this boycott. I was asked by you to serve as your spokesman." Then he added, "I want it to be known the length and breadth of this land that if I am stopped this movement will not stop. . . . What we are doing is just. And God is with us." The gathered people responded by spontaneously breaking into song, including hymns and "My country 'tis of thee, sweet land of liberty, of thee I sing."

It was the terrorist bombing and King's mature and challenging response to it that effectively began to push the Montgomery story beyond the confines of the African-American press and the local newspapers into the nation's mainstream mass media—and into the consciousness (and consciences) of hundred of thousands of its citizens, irrespective of color.

Meanwhile, the white defenders of Montgomery continued to misread the times and the people they were dealing with. Shortly after the dynamite attack on King's house, a bomb was thrown into the front yard of MIA treasurer and movement stalwart E. D. Nixon. Two weeks later 11,000 white people gathered in Montgomery for a White Citizens Council rally, where they cheered the mayor and police chief for holding the line in the cause of bus segregation. Perhaps encouraged by their own mass meeting, the city officials decided to ask a grand jury to indict nearly 100 leaders of the MIA on charges of conspiracy. That broadside approach and the refusal of the MIA leadership to be intimidated by it only intensified the national media interest in Montgomery and in King.

The first time that the Montgomery story appeared on the front page of the internationally respected *New York Times* and *New York Herald Tribune* was when these papers reported the mass meeting held the evening after the leaders were arrested, and immediately bailed out, on the conspiracy charge. Readers around the world were able to catch the spirit of determined, nonviolent resistance as thousands of boycotters gathered to hear the news from the courtroom and to stand in solidarity with their leaders. Thus the nation received King's message: "This is not a war between the white and the Negro but a conflict between justice and injustice." Expanding his vision to include the largest possible participation, King went on, "If our victory is won—and it will be won—it will be a victory for Negroes, a victory for justice, a victory for free people, and a victory for democracy." In a sense, there were hundreds of thousands of distant listeners as he proclaimed, "If we are arrested every day, if we are exploited every day, if we are trampled over every day, don't ever let anyone pull you so low as to hate them. We must use the weapon of love."

For the first time, the world could look at the black people of the South and see more than a community of powerless victims. Now there were black people taking the initiative to redefine their future. They showed a new set of faces, lifted a new chorus of voices to the world like those of the grandmother who, when asked about whether she was tired from a long day of working and walking, replied, "My feets is tired, but my soul is rested."

The nation began to respond in a variety of ways. The proprietor of Sadie's Beauty Shop in the black community of Gastonia, North Carolina, took up a collection in her shop for Montgomery's walkers. The first African-American winner of the Nobel Peace Prize, Ralph Bunche, who served as an official of the United Nations, wrote to praise and encourage King and the people of the movement: "Your patient determination, your wisdom and quiet courage are constituting an inspiring chapter in the history of human dignity." In hundreds of black churches across the country the combination of praying and organizing produced scenes like the one in Concord Baptist Church in Brooklyn, New York, where a collection of $4,000 was taken up for Montgomery in trash cans and cake boxes after the collection plates were filled.

This vital connection between King and Montgomery's church-based movement and the black church network throughout the nation was crucial in transforming the nation after World War II. For instance, supplementing the news that came from black newspapers and magazines like *Jet, Ebony,* and *Sepia,* as well as from the newly attentive white-owned media, black churches were everywhere, and they served as a massive network for information and mobilization regarding Montgomery. Other committed groups—the skycaps at Newark airport and some longshoremen in San Francisco, for example—made their own contributions, sometimes just an hour's pay. In the course of that winter a most appropriate gift came to Montgomery from a retired licensed practical nurse in Milwaukee who said she was not well and temporarily "short on money," but sent "a slightly used comfortable pair of shoes" that she thought might be useful to one of the walking women. Eventually, more than 7,000 individual letters and gifts came from around the nation and from overseas. Poets, scholars, students, community organizers, maids, pastors, laborers, union locals, and scores of "Committee(s) to Aid the People of Montgomery" communicated with the MIA, and many organizations sent delegates to Montgomery.

King and the movement attracted the attention of two of the most important religiously based pacifist groups in the country: the Fellowship of Reconciliation (FOR) and the American Friends Service Committee, better known as Quakers. Many of their members had hoped and worked for a long time to see Mahatma Gandhi's religiously inspired organizing combined with the courageous, nonviolent spirit of Jesus in the cause of racial justice and equality in the United States. Though predominantly white, they were often joined and even led by a number of African Americans, such as Howard and Sue Thurman, Benjamin Mays, Mordecai Johnson, and Bayard Rustin, the radical Quaker and peace activist. Indeed, when Montgomery broke into the mainstream news, the national chairman of the FOR was Charles Lawrence, a 1936 Morehouse College graduate who was then teaching sociology at Brooklyn College in New York. Lawrence, a firm, articulate, and jovial believer in the nonviolent struggle for justice, wrote to King as soon as he saw the newspaper reports on the post-indictment mass meeting and claimed that he found the stories "among the most thrilling documents I have ever read." He wrote, "Who knows? Providence may have given the Negroes of Montgomery the historic mission of demonstrating to the world the practical power of Christianity, the unmatched vitality of a nonviolent loving approach to social protest."

Black boycotters were continually harassed by Montgomery police, and 24 ministers were arrested and jailed.

Inspired by such grand hopes, Lawrence and his FOR colleagues sent their national field secretary, Glenn Smiley, on an exploratory visit to Montgomery that winter. Smiley, a white Texan who was an ordained minister in the Southern Methodist Church, had been involved with the Fellowship since the early 1940s and had been a conscientious objector on religious grounds during World War II. According to Lawrence's instructions, Smiley's FOR mission in Montgomery would be "primarily that of finding out what those of you who are involved directly would have those of us who are 'on the outside' do."

Meanwhile, Rustin, one of the best known activists in the pacifist movement, also went independently to offer his services to King and the Montgomery struggle. A personable, brilliant, nonviolent strategist and writer, Rustin did not, unfortunately, stay long in Montgomery. Ironically, in the eyes of some of the MIA officers, Rustin's past involvement with communist-related organizations and his prior arrest for a homosexual liaison made him more of a risk than Smiley. Nevertheless, both men helped King on what he later called his "pilgrimage to nonviolence," introducing him to leading religious pacifists, such as Howard Thurman and Harry Emerson Fosdick; introducing him to the classic published writings on nonviolence, such as Fosdick's *Hope of the World;* and assisting the MIA in developing its own training workshops in nonviolence. Rustin, in particular, helped King prepare important articles on the Montgomery struggle for a number of religious journals.

By the end of the winter of 1956, as the boycott moved into its fourth month, King's picture had appeared on the cover of a number of national magazines, and his name and message were familiar in many other parts of the world. He carried the message across the nation, his powerful baritone voice reverberating in scores of large churches, on college and university campuses, in municipal auditoriums, at conventions of the NAACP and the National Urban League (a civil rights and economic betterment organization founded in 1911), at fraternal and religious conventions, even at a black funeral directors' convention.

Wherever he went, King's message was essentially the same. He announced and embodied the rise of a "new Negro" in the South, saying everywhere that "you can't understand the Montgomery situation unless you understand that the Negro has a new sense of dignity, a new realization of his own worth." Grounded in the emerging mode of self-affirmation among the black people of Montgomery, King consistently proclaimed, "It may be that . . . in the capital of the Confederacy, the . . . ideal of freedom in America and in the southland can be born." Neither a struggle for bus desegregation or for "civil rights" was an adequate description of their fight, King said. The message could not have been clearer than in a letter he sent that spring to a group of Northern white supporters: "Our struggle here is not merely a struggle for Montgomery but it is really a struggle for the whole of America." (Actually, he did not confine his attention to America, for everywhere that King spoke he reminded his audience that the black minority of America was part of a worldwide majority of

Many civil rights activists were inspired by the teachings of Mohandas Gandhi, the leader of India's independence movement who advocated nonviolent protest.

darker-hued people, people involved in freedom's ferment from Bandung, Indonesia, to Capetown, South Africa, to Vietnam.)

By the fall of 1956 Montgomery had become the unmistakable symbol of transformation in the nation, a symbol of its African-American citizens and its Southern-based traditions of legal segregation, white domination, and the subversion of democratic hope. That symbol belonged to all the licensed practical nurses, the maids and skycaps, the scholars and Nobel laureates, the prisoners, students, artists, and pastors who would eventually create their own versions of Montgomery across the nation.

By this time the Montgomery movement had also provided a crucial set of opportunities for King and his coworkers to experiment with Gandhian nonviolent action (or "passive resistance," as King sometimes described it) on behalf of freedom and justice. King could now announce with confidence, "We in Montgomery have discovered a method that can

be used by the Negroes in their fight for political and economic equality. . . .
We fight injustice with passive resistance. . . . Mohandas Gandhi . . . used it
to topple the British military machine. . . . Let's now use this method in the
United States."

At the same time, while he increasingly referred to Gandhi, King
kept returning to his fundamental grounding in the black church experience. "The spirit of passive resistance came to me from the Bible," he said,
"from the teachings of Jesus. The techniques came from Gandhi." Sum-
ming up what the events in Montgomery meant for a religiously sensitive
region and nation, King continued to affirm that "This is a spiritual movement, depending on moral and spiritual forces."

But such a spiritual vision did not exclude the use of practical methods. For instance, the white authorities' unwillingness to negotiate and the
continued harassment and violence directed at the black community compelled the MIA leaders to take their struggle into the courts. In consulta-
tion with the local and national NAACP lawyers, the MIA initiated a legal
suit to challenge the constitutionality of Montgomery's segregated bus system. They had moved far beyond the initial quest for "a more humane
form of segregation." Now they were challenging the Jim Crow transportation system itself. The case was identified as *Gayle* v. *Browder* (1956). And
when the U.S. Supreme Court ruled in favor of the black citizens of
Montgomery, it was clear the South was about to change forever.

The Court's ruling in *Gayle* v. *Browder* was announced on November
13, 1956, but no one knew when the official papers of notification would
reach Montgomery. The city commission refused to allow the bus company
to make any changes in its practices until the court documents actually
arrived in their offices. But the people of the movement prepared themselves for the next phase of the journey they had begun on December 5,
1955. On the night when the Supreme Court decision was announced, a
caravan of 40 cars of Klan members drove through the city's black neighborhoods. But no one ran into their houses. No one pulled down the
shades. Instead, many "New Negroes" stood and watched calmly. Some
even waved to the disconcerted white-robed visitors, and soon the visitors
drove away.

The next night there were two mass meetings to accommodate all the
people full of courage who had come to give thanks for the past and plan
for the future. It was natural that the MIA executive committee called on
King to address the meetings that night. Speaking at Holt Street Church,

where they had begun together, King said, "These eleven months have not all been easy. . . . We have lived with this protest so long that we have learned the meaning of sacrifice and suffering. But somehow we feel that our suffering is redemptive." Forever the teacher, King felt that he had to encourage the people to consider what it would mean to "press on" to their next steps "in the spirit of the movement." For him, two elements were crucial. One was the need to avoid arrogance as they made their victorious return to the buses. Taking on a personal tone, he said to the people, "I would be terribly disappointed if anybody goes back to the buses bragging about, we, the Negroes, have won a victory over the white people." Instead, King called on them to remember the need to open both the struggle and the victory beyond racial lines. So he said that when the legal papers finally arrived, "it will be a victory for justice and a victory for good-will and a victory for the forces of light. So let us not limit this decision to a

On December 21, 1956, Rosa Parks takes her hard-won seat in the front of a recently desegregated Montgomery city bus.

victory for Negroes. Let us go back to the buses in all humility and with gratitude to the Almighty God for making this [court] decision possible."

King quickly made it clear that "humility" did not mean fearful acquiescence, going to the back of the bus when there were empty seats in front. No, he told them, it was imperative that they sit wherever seats were available. "We have a duty to ourselves for our self-respect and before the Almighty God to stand up for our freedom." So he was proposing that they, like Rosa Parks before them, take a stand by sitting with dignity and with a sense of humane good will. Specifically, he called on them to refuse to be drawn by white opponents into fights or arguments. "What I'm saying to you this evening is that you can be courageous and yet nonviolent." Invoking the spirit of the movement, King declared, "If we go back on the buses and somehow become so weak that when somebody strikes us we gonna strike them back, or when somebody says an insulting word to us we gonna do the same thing, we will destroy the spirit of our movement."

Even at such a high point in their struggle, King knew that he was pressing his people toward a fiercely demanding discipline. He said, "I know it's hard" but kept pushing: "the strong man is the man . . . who can stand up for his rights and yet not hit back."

King knew they were on a dangerous path. They were poised at a crucial moment in history, a moment that required disciplined courage and disciplined love, especially in the light of the South's long history of violence against black attempts to gain justice. Finally, King faced his people with the ultimate encouragement—his willingness to sacrifice his own life. Normally not given to this kind of self-focus, it was a clear sign that he saw the moment as a moment of crisis, one similar to that January night on his bombed-out porch. So he said to the visibly moved assembly:

> I'm not telling you something that I don't live. [Someone yelled, "That's right!"] I'm aware of the fact that the Klu Klux Klan is riding in Montgomery. I'm aware of the fact that a week never passes that somebody's not telling me to get out of town, or that I'm going to be killed next place I move. But I don't have any guns in my pockets. I don't have any guards on my side.
>
> But I have the God of the Universe on my side. I'm serious about that. I can walk the streets of Montgomery without fear. I don't worry about a thing. They can bomb my house. They can kill my body. But they can never kill the spirit of freedom that is in my people.

A maintenance worker removes a segregation sign from a city bus in Dallas, Texas. The Montgomery bus boycott led to a 1956 Supreme Court ruling that declared segregated bus seating unconstitutional.

All through this remarkable testimony of encouragement, the people at Holt Street were deeply engaged with King, offering their vocal encouragement, sharing their applause. And when he was finished with those last words, they burst out in even more applause, clapping for him, for themselves, for the victory, for the children who would continue to rekindle the spirit of freedom in the days to come.

Finally, on December 20, the Supreme Court mandate made its way to Montgomery, affirming the people and their audacious struggle. The next morning a restrained but happy group, including King, Abernathy, and Smiley, boarded the first desegregated bus, beginning a new phase of the long journey toward freedom and justice for all.

CHAPTER 3

OLD ORDER, NEW ORDER

By the time the victory was won in Montgomery, the struggle had lasted for more than a year. People had walked for more than a year, shared rides for more than a year, attended weekly mass meetings for more than a year, planned new strategies for more than a year. They had learned new songs, sung old ones, offered up more than a year's prayers, waited through more than a year of long nights wondering if the sound of a dynamite blast would shatter the quiet again, determined countless times not to give in to white threats for more than a year. They had explained to growing children for more than a year what all the excitement was about, and how everything was being done for them. And out beyond Montgomery those 381 days provided time enough for the unique experience to embed itself in the consciousness of the nation.

All along the way there were dramatic, compelling new events, bombings, indictments, rallies in other cities, and courtroom trials reminding people, especially black people, that the Montgomery movement was alive. Black folks had stuck together and grown together in the longest sustained campaign for justice that the nation had ever seen.

And, of course, the movement's prime symbol, Martin Luther King, Jr., seemed to be everywhere, proclaiming and exemplifying the emergence of a new people and a new time. By the time the legal victory was announced in Montgomery, it appeared that King was right: It was far more than a victory for the black walkers of Montgomery (although *that* victory certainly needed to be savored and celebrated), and wherever people claimed the fruits of the long ordeal, a powerful energy of hope and a sense of new possibilities appeared.

Sometimes the Montgomery connections to other places in the nation was obvious. In cities such as Mobile and Birmingham, Alabama, and near-

The success of the Montgomery bus boycotters inspired blacks throughout the South to become actively involved in local politics. In Memphis, students eagerly anticipated a visit from Martin Luther King, Jr., in 1959.

61

by Tallahassee, Florida, ministers tried to repeat the Montgomery success with their own bus boycotts. In January 1957 King and the Fellowship of Reconciliation brought together some 60 representatives of these and other boycott movements to a conference in Atlanta. They discussed the possibility of forming a regional organization based on the Montgomery experience. Before the summer of 1957 was over, King and his fellow black ministers had established the Southern Christian Leadership Conference (SCLC).

The major early accomplishments of SCLC were the sponsorship of several conferences and organizing, with Bayard Rustin and A. Philip Randolph, a "prayer pilgrimage" of about 20,000 people in Washington, D.C., who were calling for civil rights legislation. SCLC also hoped to undertake a "Crusade for Citizenship," projected as a massive Southwide voter registration campaign based in the black churches. Due to lack of personnel, planning, and finances, this campaign never materialized.

Even with its provocative founding announcement that "we have come to redeem the soul of America" and the predictable choice of King as president, the mostly Baptist group was not, however, able to focus and mobilize the new energies in the ways that King, his Alabama comrades, and his Northern allies had hoped. This was partly because the approximately 100 men (there were only men in mainstream black church leadership) who formed the core of the SCLC were only a small minority of the black ministers of the South. And, besides, SCLC's ministers had had no real experience in forming a regional organization that would be both flexible and open to new strategies yet also structured enough to mount a sustained challenge to the system of legal segregation.

So for a number of years after the Montgomery victory, the energies that were released there had to

In Tallahassee, Florida, black residents repeated the success of the Montgomery bus boycotters, staging a seven-month boycott that integrated city buses in 1956.

be channeled into less obvious places than the Southern black churches that had anchored the celebrated boycott. As a result, the expansion of the Southern freedom movement depended on unlikely groups of people, emerging from unexpected places.

For instance, there was the teenager John Lewis, a short, slightly built, slow-speaking country boy from Troy, Alabama, who had first heard King's pre-boycott preaching on a local black radio station. The unassuming but religiously rooted Lewis had been training himself for his own calling by preaching to the livestock in his family's yard, and baptizing some of them too. Regardless of his unconventional training and practice congregation, Lewis knew that there was work for him to do, and King and the people of Montgomery were his models. Throughout the post-Montgomery decade, John Lewis took that work and those models into some of the most dangerous frontiers of the Southern-based struggle for freedom, accumulating many scars and much honor in the process. As a Freedom Rider in 1961, Lewis rode buses throughout the South, testing the law that made segregated buses and station facilities illegal. He became the first Freedom Rider to meet with violence when he was struck by some white men as he attempted to go through the white entrance to the Rock Hill, South Carolina, Greyhound bus station.

In the same way, few people would have predicted that a matronly, middle-aged black South Carolinian named Septima Poinsette Clark would be one of the most effective carriers of Montgomery's best spirit. In her 50s when the victory was won, the Charleston woman was not too old to be a "new Negro." A veteran teacher in the public school system of Charleston, she had led important struggles for the equalizing of salaries for black and white teachers.

Then, on April 19, 1956, a law was passed prohibiting state and city employees from having an affiliation with any civil rights group, including the NAACP. Clark refused to obey the law and lost her job. She now joined forces with the white Southerners who had founded the Highlander Folk School in the mountains of eastern Tennessee. Highlander was established in the 1930s as a nontraditional educational center to encourage local citizens and others to build a more just and democratic society across racial lines.

At Highlander the soft-spoken but iron-willed Clark created a program based on work she had been doing for decades. She called it Citizenship Education, and it involved an informal but carefully crafted workshop combination of storytelling, political analysis, American and

African-American history, religious education, autobiographical sharing, careful study of arcane voter registration laws and forms, and much singing and mutual encouragement. With such deceptively simple methods, Clark and her expanding group of coworkers performed an almost unbelievable task. They helped thousands of marginally literate (and sometimes illiterate) black people not only learn to read and write their way to voter registration skills, but also to teach others, and to become committed believers in the freedom movement.

By that time many people had discovered that the path blazed by Rosa Parks, Martin Luther King, Jr., and the Montgomery boycotters was not meant to be duplicated exactly. That was clear not only in efforts of people like John Lewis and Septima Clark. It could also be seen in the failed attempts to build Montgomery copycat boycotts in places like Mobile and Tallahassee, failures that inspired people to search for other methods. Indeed when King had declared near the close of the Montgomery boycott that "nothing can kill the spirit of my people," he probably understood that the spirit needed to take many different forms.

That spirit was seen, for instance, in the fiery determination of Fred Shuttlesworth, the Birmingham pastor who became a staunch comrade to Martin King in the next stages of the Southern freedom movement. A contrast to King in almost every conceivable way, Shuttlesworth was a native of Alabama's backwoods—a wiry, volatile, and gritty man. Before he answered the inner call to the Christian ministry, he had been a truck driver, cement worker, and operator of the family's whiskey still. Indeed, he was just the kind of utterly courageous, sharp-tongued, quick-tempered believer in nonviolence that the movement needed. Though profoundly inspired by King and Montgomery, Shuttlesworth was his own man. When white-led governments across the South responded to black assertiveness by banning established organizations such as the NAACP, Shuttlesworth's independence proved invaluable.

In Alabama the white authorities formally blamed the national organization and its local branches for organizing an illegal boycott by black residents of Montgomery and used that as their excuse for outlawing the organization in the state. The state demanded its membership lists (a demand that the NAACP managed successfully to resist for the eight years that it took to get the state action reversed in federal courts). Just a few days after the NAACP ban went into effect, Fred Shuttlesworth angered the local authorities when he formed a new, replacement organization from his

NAACP members march to the Florida state capitol in Tallahassee. Since the 1940s, the civil rights agenda in the South had incorporated demands for fair employment and voting rights.

Birmingham base, calling it the Alabama Christian Movement for Human Rights (ACMHR). Led essentially (and somewhat autocratically) by Shuttlesworth, the ACMHR became one of the most vital affiliates of the Southern Christian Leadership Conference, temporarily providing a mass movement–oriented substitute for the NAACP and eventually carrying the spirit of Montgomery to another level of confrontation. The ACMHR fought against bus segregation in December 1956 and October 1958, using direct-action tactics. It also tried to integrate Birmingham schools and train stations in 1957.

In other states—such as Mississippi and Florida—courageous NAACP officials and those who tried to stand with them were sometimes run out of the state or assassinated. On Christmas night 1951, Harry T. Moore, executive secretary of NAACP branches in Florida, and his wife were killed when their house was bombed in Mims, Florida. Shuttlesworth himself was subjected to everything from midday beatings by mobs of white segregationists on the city streets to the nighttime bombing of his house and church. The attacks intensified after the intrepid pastor insisted on personally desegregating the Birmingham city buses and on trying to enroll his children in an all-white school in the stubbornly segregated city school system.

All over the South there were black parents and children like the Shuttlesworths who were determined to take the historic words of the *Brown* decision and turn them into sturdy actions of desegregation. In the more than 2,000 Southern school districts that were affected by the court's decision, most often it was the black community that took the initiative in converting a legal decision into a social reality.

Indeed, public opinion polls revealed that 80 percent of white Southerners were opposed to school desegregation in the immediate post-*Brown* period. Although the terms of opposition were framed in various ways (such as distaste over "sitting next to niggers," or "*they* can't come into *our* school," or "God didn't intend us to be together," or a thousand other home-brewed formulations), so much finally came down to the basic truth that South Carolina governor James Byrnes had expressed. If taken seriously, desegregation marked "the beginning of the end of civilization in the South" as white people—especially privileged white people—had known it. In the same way, there was no room for misinterpreting the so-called "Southern manifesto" that had been signed in March 1956 by 90 Southern members of the House of Representatives and by all of the senators except Estes Kefauver and Albert Gore of Tennessee and Senate majority leader Lyndon Johnson. In this document these respected senators and representatives denied that the Supreme Court had a right to rule on racial issues in the realm of public education, as it had in the *Brown* decision, and called upon their constituents to disobey the court's order, offering "massive resistance" to the ruling.

In addition, the person who might have been expected to provide some firm guidance to the nation in this crucial time of transition was offering a version of his own resistance. The widely admired military hero Dwight D. Eisenhower had been elected President in 1952 and again in 1956. He probably had more leverage to lead the nation down the path of peaceful change than any other public figure, but he never really came to the aid of African Americans. Rather, the President chose to condemn what he called "the extremists on both sides" of the school desegregation question, thereby equating courageous children and their communities who were working for democratic change with men and women who defied the Supreme Court, dynamited buildings, and assassinated leaders.

Though Eisenhower never made a clear public statement of opposition to the Court's action in *Brown*, neither did he ever publicly support it as an act of democratic justice and moral rightness. Having had no experience with black people outside of superior/subordinate relationships in the military, Eisenhower privately said more than once, "I am convinced that the Supreme Court decision set back progress in the South at least fifteen years." He felt that "forcing" desegregation would raise white resistance. But as the nature of the battle for desegregation progressed, Eisenhower was forced to take action on behalf of the federal government.

Faced with such a range of opposition—midnight bombers, an uncommitted President, members of Congress urging "massive resistance," and the Supreme Court's own ambiguous 1955 call for school districts to move to implement the *Brown* decision not by any certain date but "with all deliberate speed"—it would not have been surprising if Southern blacks had given up the quest for desegregated schools. But they were constantly reminding each other that "we've come too far to turn back."

Children, ranging in ages from 6 to 17, were on the front lines of this phase of the struggle. In hundreds of schools across the South, the children had to face hatred, ignorance, and fear. As they arrived at newly desegregated schools, they had to face screaming, cursing, threatening presences of white men, children, and women who had appointed themselves as protectors of the social and educational bastions of white supremacy.

Still, the black children went into the schools—sometimes to the accompaniment of white rioting in the streets, sometimes under the protection of federal marshals or troops. One white teacher from Tennessee remembered the reception the pioneering black children met in her school, a typical experience:

As an army general, Dwight D. Eisenhower (center) was accustomed to racial segregation in the military. But as President, after much prodding, he finally stood behind the Supreme Court ruling outlawing school segregation.

Eggs smashed on their books, ink smeared on their clothes, in the lockers, knives flourished in their presence, nails tossed in their faces and spiked in their seats. Vulgar words constantly whispered in their ears. "If you come back to school, I'll cut your guts out!" could be heard in the halls. . . .

Although they often felt desolate and terrified in such hostile situations, the black children also heard other voices and knew they were not alone: "We've come too far together to turn back." "If God be for us, who can be against us?" Of course, they knew those voices of hope better than the threatening voices in the halls. The parents, pastors, extended family members, and church and community people who had often gone with them right up to the doors of the unwelcoming schools were now bonded with them more deeply than ever before.

Besides, in almost every such situation of bravery and risk there was someone in the supportive community like Grandma India, who was the special confidant in the home of Melba Pattillo, one of the teenagers chosen in 1957 to pioneer the desegregation of Central High School in Little Rock, Arkansas. Having helped to nurse Melba through a near fatal illness after her birth, it was Grandma India who regularly encouraged the gifted young woman. Melba recorded in her diary what her grandmother said: "Now you see the reason God spared your life. You're supposed to carry this banner for our people." Several days later, in the midst of her early Central High experience, Melba wrote in her diary (where she kept "messages to God," as she called them): "Okay, God, so Grandma is right. . . . It's my turn to carry the banner. Please help me to do thy will."

Eventually, all the possibilities and complications of the post-Montgomery struggles for a desegregated nation seemed to gather around Melba Pattillo's new school, Little Rock's Central High. Little Rock was considered a city that was reasonably open to the powerful surges of change that were mounting in the South, and in 1954 it had been the first Southern city to respond positively to the *Brown* decision. Less than a week after the decision was announced, the Little Rock school board declared its intention to voluntarily desegregate its public schools, beginning with the 2,000-student Central High, located in a working-class white neighborhood. However, it was not until 1957 that the board announced that it would actually begin the desegregation process—on a rather timid level—that fall. Then 75 students volunteered to lead the way. Of those, 25 were chosen. The all-white school board, worried about a brewing politically inspired white reaction, soon pared the number down to nine. Six young women and three young men were chosen to "carry the banner." Melba Pattillo was among them.

Unfortunately, the white community of Little Rock and the state of Arkansas once again lacked the kind of courageous moral leadership that would have helped guide them. Instead the confused and searching citizens were subjected to the mercurial and election-driven performance of

Armed soldiers confront white students at Central High School in Little Rock. Because of the serious challenge to federal authority in Arkansas, President Eisenhower sent 1,000 U.S. Army troops to protect the 9 black students who had defied white protests and threats of violence to enroll at the school.

Governor Orville Faubus. A racial "moderate" in pre-1954 Southern white terms, he had become convinced that in order to be reelected, he had to respond to the worst fears of the white parents and politicians who were busy galvanizing opposition to the school board's modest desegregation plan. This led to the spectacle of Faubus calling out the Arkansas National Guard that fall to block the way of Melba Pattillo and the other eight black students as they—with amazing poise—moved past a crowd of screaming adults and young people and tried to enter Central High.

Such a use of state troops to resist a U.S. Supreme Court order, carried out in front of national network television cameras, finally pushed Eisenhower to action. But his initial attempt to use his personal powers of persuasion on Faubus turned out to be too little too late and served only to help heighten the crisis. Ten days after the beginning of the Little Rock crisis, Eisenhower summoned Faubus to a private conference. The governor left his conversation with the President to return to Little Rock and pull away the Arkansas National Guard, leaving only the local police to deal with the constantly expanding crowd of white adult opponents at the school building. Their hysterical calls for resistance to integration finally erupted into violence against several black journalists. At the same time there were

Army vehicles transported the black students to and from Little Rock's Central High School, where they faced daily acts of harassment and intimidation in the hallways, classrooms, and lunchroom.

reckless threats from the mob to lynch one or more of the black students. The scenes of white crowds surging against the overwhelmed and under-committed local police moved across the nation's television screens. (The medium was new, and the black struggle for freedom in the South was its first major ongoing story.) Many people also saw the electrifying image of Elizabeth Eckford, another of the black students in Little Rock, accidentally cut off from the rest of the group of students, surrounded by the hostile mob, moving in silent, terrified dignity, finally joined by a tall white woman, Grace Lorch, who stood by her side and then helped her board a bus to safety.

Eisenhower finally did what he had pledged never to do: send federal troops to Little Rock "to aid in the execution of federal law," he said to the nation. But he also sent more than a thousand riot-trained troops from the 101st Airborne Division to protect the right of nine young citizens to make use of the opportunity that the Supreme Court had guaranteed to them.

The Little Rock pioneers stayed the course, managed to live through an academic year of hateful taunts and actual assaults, managed also to find a few friends. For a while each student was accompanied in the school by a soldier, but these military companions could not go into locker rooms, lavatories, classrooms, the cafeteria, and other spaces that had become danger spots. There came a time when one of the nine, Minnie Jean Brown, finally gave in to the deep frustration they were all feeling and one day poured her bowl of chili on the head of a persistent tormentor. Her unexpected action evoked a spontaneous round of applause from the black cafeteria workers, but it also led to a suspension from school, and Minnie Jean finished her academic year in New York City. Meanwhile the other students continued, making their way to the end of Central High's school year, carrying the banner—and the pain—all the way.

Crucial to their endurance was the community support that they found, not only in all the Grandma Indias, but also in Daisy Bates, the chairperson of the local NAACP chapter and the publisher, with her husband, of the black community's newspaper, the *Arkansas State Gazette*. The Bateses paid a heavy financial and emotional price for their unwavering commitment to the students. They were, for example, repeatedly harassed by rock-throwing motorists who attacked their home. But the couple found some consolation in the fact that their teenaged crusaders had caught the imagination and support of concerned people all over the world.

One of the best-known testimonies to this far-reaching influence and support appeared in 1958 in *Here I Stand*, the outspoken personal and political memoir of Paul Robeson, an internationally recognized African-American activist. Writing with unabashed pride and affection to the young heroes of Little Rock—and to members of their undaunted generation all over the South—Robeson declared in his memoir:

> Dear children of Little Rock—you and your parents and the Negro people of your community have lifted our hearts and renewed our resolve that full freedom shall now be ours. You are the pride and glory of our people, and my heart sings warm and tender with love for you.

Then, lifting the children to another level, the great artist and freedom worker added these words: "You are our children, but the peoples of the whole world rightly claim you too. They have seen your faces, and the faces of those who hate you, and they are on your side."

Robeson, King, and Daisy Bates, however, surely realized that their positions did not represent the thoughts and actions of all African Americans. They knew that there were many people in both the South and the North who were not convinced that a just and humane new nation could be born on this bloody ground. These reluctant unbelievers simply could not convince themselves that American democracy could ever become a reality for black people.

As a matter of fact, even as the Little Rock struggle was going on in the 1957–58 academic year, in Monroe, North Carolina, a rather different scenario was developing. Ex-Marine Robert Williams, who had been so ecstatic with hope at the time of the *Brown* decision, had returned to his hometown of Monroe after the Korean War. He soon became president of the local branch of the NAACP and also became convinced that his military training provided a better alternative for dealing with the terrorists of the Klan and other white groups than King's way of nonviolent resistance. With the help of the National Rifle Association, Williams created a rifle club within his NAACP branch and began talking of the need to "meet lynching with lynching." But by the middle of 1959 Williams found himself attacked and disowned by the national NAACP organization and hounded as a fugitive by local and national law enforcement agencies. Two years later, he was forced to flee the country altogether as a result of trumped-up kidnapping charges. Eventually he became an exile from the land that once inspired his hope, finding political asylum in Cuba, which had just undergone its own socialist revolution. He later went to China and then the East African nation of Tanzania before returning to America almost a decade later.

Nevertheless, Williams's demand for an alternative to nonviolent resistance did not end with his departure. His calls for armed self-defense and physical retaliation were familiar themes in the traditions of black American resistance. Indeed, even then an important variation on this theme was rising up in the northern cities of the nation.

When all eyes seemed to be on Montgomery, in the black communities of Detroit, New York, Chicago, Los Angeles, and elsewhere a growing number of young black men, impeccably dressed in suits and bow ties, and young women, wrapped in long, flowing white dresses, became a regular part of the urban landscape. These quiet, dignified, disciplined black folk were practicing Muslims—members of the Nation of Islam (NOI). The NOI was founded by an obscure self-styled prophet named W. D. Fard in the 1930s. Fard and his handpicked successor, Elijah Poole (who would later take the name Elijah Muhammad), preached a modified version of Islam. It combined claims of black racial supremacy (such as the idea that black people were the original people and whites were "devils" invented by a mad scientist named Yacub) with elements of the orthodox Islamic tradition and borrowed heavily from the style and structure of black Christian churches. Despite their reputation for being a radical sect, the NOI promoted fairly conservative ideas and values. It sought to "uplift" the race by establishing black-owned businesses and "teaching" black ghetto dwellers the importance of discipline, self-help, and cleanliness. It imposed strict rules about personal behavior: alcohol, drugs, tobacco, gambling, dancing, adultery, premarital sex, profanity, or watching movies with sex or "coarse speech," for example, were simply not allowed. The NOI even impressed black conservative George Schuyler, managing editor of the New York office of the black-owned *Pittsburgh Courier,* who praised them for their values and moral vision. "Mr. Muhammad may be a rogue and a charlatan," wrote Schuyler in 1959, "but when anybody can get tens of thousands of Negroes to practice economic solidarity, respect their women, alter their atrocious diet, give up liquor, stop crime, juvenile delinquency and adultery, he is doing more for the Negro's welfare than any current Negro leader I know." Although the NOI officially stayed out of politics, focusing its energies on the spiritual uplift of African Americans and offering an alternative to the "white man's religion," it did practice self-defense and did not shy away from violence. During the 1930s in Detroit, for example, Black Muslims, as members of the NOI were known, attracted attention during a bloody shootout with police. And under Fard's leadership, the NOI even established a paramilitary organization known as the Fruit of Islam. They kept order at big gatherings, served as bodyguards for "the Messenger" (Muhammad), and were trained to defend NOI institutions at any cost.

The NOI remained a fairly small religious sect until World War II. Its membership began to increase after Elijah Muhammad and about 100 other Muslims were jailed for resisting the draft. As a result, the NOI not only garnered more national publicity but it began to recruit members from the ranks of black prisoners. One of those prisoners who discovered the Nation was Malcolm Little, whose name was changed to Malcolm X by

The Nation of Islam attracted thousands of urban blacks to the disciplined life of abstinence, prayer, and black self-determination.

Elijah Muhammad. He wrote in his autobiography that he received the X from the Nation of Islam as a symbol of his unknown African ancestry. More than any other figure, Malcolm X was responsible for turning the NOI into a national force to be reckoned with. And more than anyone else, he embodied the NOI's militant, uncompromising, and, when needed, violent image, one that would scare many white liberals and nurture a new generation of black radicals.

The son of Louisa and Earl Little—a Baptist preacher—Malcolm and his siblings experienced dramatic confrontations with racism. According to his autobiography, hooded Klansmen burned their home in Lansing, Michigan. Earl Little was killed under mysterious circumstances, welfare agencies split up the children and eventually had Louisa Little committed to a mental institution, and Malcolm was forced to live in a detention home run by a racist white couple. By the eighth grade he had left school, moved to Boston to live with his half-sister Ella, and discovered the underground world of African-American hipsters and petty criminals. His downward spiral ended in 1946, when he was sentenced to 10 years in jail for burglary.

After discovering Islam, Malcolm Little submitted to the discipline and guidance of the NOI and became a voracious reader of the Koran and the Bible. He also immersed himself in works of literature and history in the prison library. Upon his release in 1952, Malcolm X, a devoted follower of Elijah Muhammad, rose quickly within the NOI ranks, serving as minister of Harlem's Temple No. 7, where he went in 1954. He later ministered to temples in Detroit and Philadelphia. Through speaking engagements, television appearances, and by establishing *Muhammad Speaks*—the NOI's first nationally distributed newspaper—Malcolm X called America's attention to the Nation of Islam. His criticisms of civil rights leaders for advocating integration into white society instead of building black institutions and defending themselves from racist violence generated opposition from both conservatives and liberals. His opponents called him "violent," "fascist," and "racist." To those who claimed that the NOI undermined their efforts toward integration by preaching racial separatism, Malcolm responded: "It is not integration that Negroes in America want, it is human dignity."

But Malcolm showed signs of independence from the NOI line. During the mid–1950s, for example, he privately scoffed at Elijah Muhammad's interpretation of the genesis of the "white race" and seemed uncomfortable with the idea that all white people were literally devils. More significantly, Malcolm clearly disagreed with the NOI's policy of not

Elijah Muhammad helped found the Nation of Islam (NOI). He preached that white people were evil, and in 1960 he called for the creation of a separate black state in America. Generally, the NOI kept its distance from the black struggle for freedom and justice, claiming that Allah's true people— black people—ought not to forge a community with those who rejected them.

Toward the end of his life, Malcolm X rejected the Nation of Islam's message of hatred for whites and emphasized the need for black economic independence. He had gained a substantial following when he was assassinated in 1965 by black men who may have been connected to the Nation of Islam.

participating in politics. He not only believed that political mobilization was indispensable but occasionally defied the rule by supporting boycotts and other forms of protest. He had begun developing a Third World political perspective during the 1950s, when anticolonial wars and decolonization were pressing public issues. As early as 1954, Malcolm gave a speech comparing the situation in Vietnam with that of the Mau Mau rebellion against the British in colonial Kenya, framing both of these movements as uprisings of the "Darker races" creating a "Tidal Wave" against U.S. and European imperialism. Indeed, Africa remained his primary political interest outside black America: in 1959 he toured Egypt, Sudan, Nigeria, and Ghana to develop ties between African Americans and the newly independent African states.

Of course, Malcolm was not the only black leader whose politics were deeply inspired by international developments. Black people on both sides of the Atlantic reached out to each other. When Ghana won its independence, they celebrated; when CIA-backed forces assassinated Patrice Lumumba, the newly elected prime minister of the Congo, they mourned and protested. After Martin and Coretta King's visit to Ghana in 1957, Ghanaian prime minister Kwame Nkrumah grandly toured the black capital of the United States: Harlem, in New York City. Guinean president Sékou Touré followed, passing through Harlem in 1960. Perhaps the most famous sojourn of 1960 was Cuban president Fidel Castro's infamous residency at Harlem's Hotel Theresa during his visit to the United Nations. Castro brought black people face to face with an avowed socialist who extended a hand of solidarity to people of color the world over. On the other side, dozens of black activists and artists and intellectuals, seeing their fate tied up with Africa's future, left America to take up residence in Ghana. This distinguished group of expatriates included scholar and activist W. E. B. Du Bois, writer Maya Angelou, artist John Biggers, and labor organizer Vickie Garvin. And dozens of black radicals not only publicly defended the Cuban revolution but visited the island nation through groups such as the Fair Play for Cuba Committee.

African Americans had long seen themselves as part of a larger world, as more than "minorities" within the confines of the United States. But there was never a time like this, when every corner of the earth seemed engaged in a struggle for freedom, and the black freedom movement in America seemed to be at the eye of the international storm.

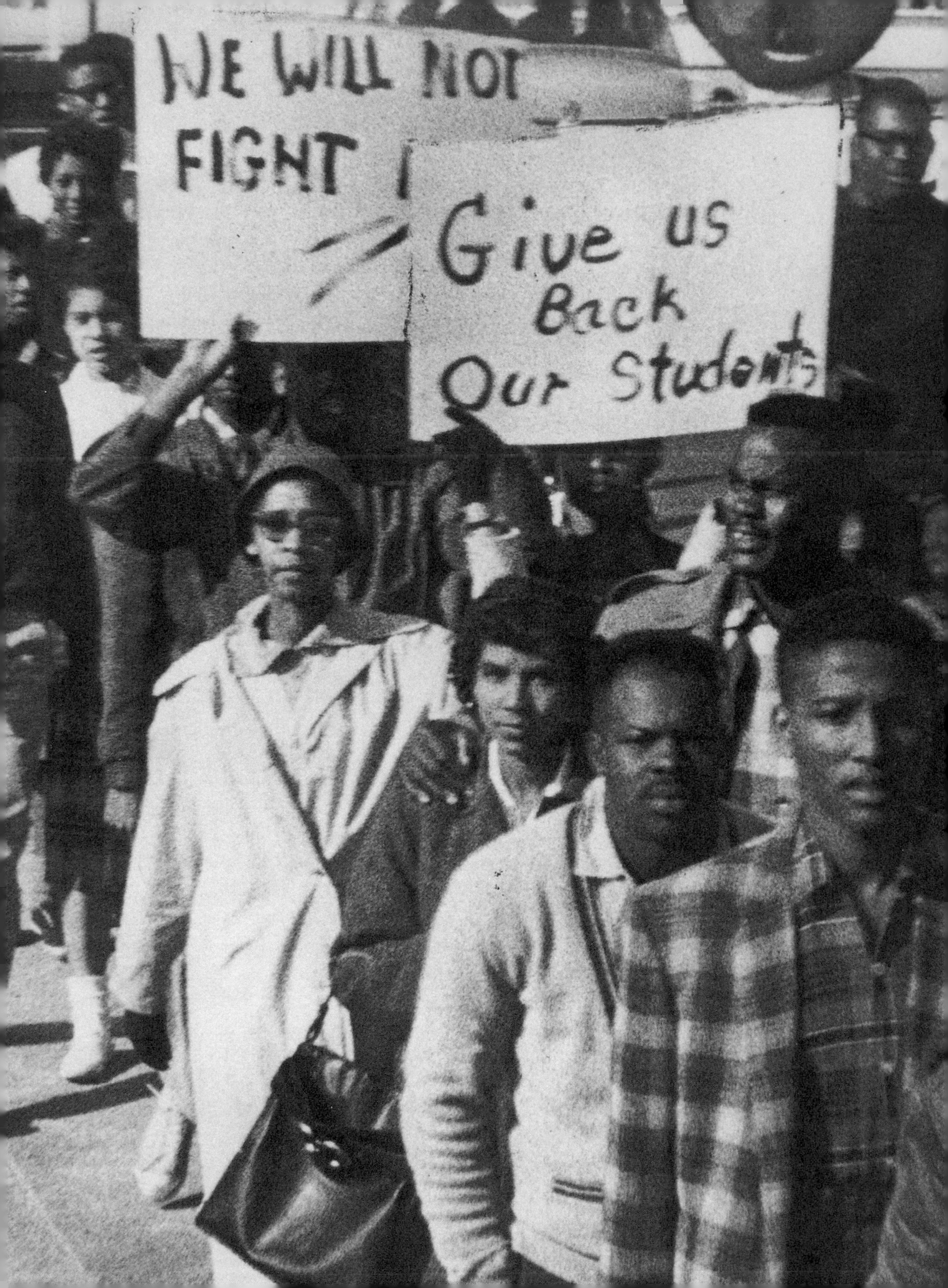
WE WILL NOT
FIGHT
Give us
Back
Our Students

CHAPTER 4

FREEDOM NOW!: THE STUDENT REVOLUTIONARIES
◇ ◇ ◇

*In March 1960,
blacks in Tallahassee
protest the arrest of
23 Florida A&M stu-
dents who had sat in
at an all-white lunch
counter. By this time,
student sit-ins had
spread from
Greensboro, North
Carolina, to 31
Southern cities.*

O n a Sunday morning late in November 1959, Martin Luther King, Jr., announced to his congregation at Dexter Avenue Baptist Church in Montgomery, Alabama, that he had decided to leave the city and return to his native Atlanta. The major reason was the need to connect himself more firmly to the Southern Christian Leadership Conference, which had been headquartered in Atlanta since its founding in 1957. In the years since its establishment, SCLC had been having a hard time getting organized. In the statement he made to the Dexter congregation that Sunday, King seemed to be trying to rally himself, his organization, and the larger developing freedom movement to a new state of activity. He said, "The time has come for a broad, bold advance of the Southern campaign for equality. . . . Not only will it include a stepped-up campaign of voter registration, but a full-scale assault will be made upon discrimination and segregation in all forms. . . . We must employ new methods of struggle involving the masses of our people."

In this "bold advance" King envisioned SCLC as a crucial force, and he was convinced that a great deal of the energy that was needed would come from black young people. Indeed, King said, "We must train our youth . . . in the techniques of social change through nonviolent resistance." It is likely that King was envisioning a youth movement that would be firmly based in the SCLC organization. But by the time King moved to Atlanta in January 1960, SCLC had not yet done anything to organize a youth movement. Fortunately, the young people were not waiting. Beginning independently from several Southern bases, an ever-expanding nonviolent army of black young people and their white allies began to put an indelible mark on the 1960s.

On the same Sunday night that Montgomery's black community was formally saying good-bye to Martin and Coretta King, the newest actors in the freedom drama were preparing for their own arrival on the stage. On January 31, 1960, at North Carolina Agricultural and Technical College (known as A&T), one of the South's many black colleges, four freshmen decided to move from words to deeds. Ezell Blair, Jr., Joseph McNeil, Franklin McClain, and David Richmond decided that they were going to confront one of the most demeaning symbols of segregation: the all-white lunch counter at the local Woolworth's department store. Like all the chain stores in the South, the Greensboro store accepted the money of its African-American customers at the various merchandise counters, but the lunch counter was a different story. Black people were not permitted to sit for a snack, a meal, or even a drink of water. Usually, such segregationist practices were enforced by local ordinances, state laws, and coercion by whites acting almost out of habit. Whites considered public space theirs to control and define, and they were especially sensitive about public eating places, where white employees might be perceived as serving blacks (as opposed to merely accepting their payments at other store counters).

The young men from A&T planned to go into Woolworth's on Monday morning, February 1, shop for some small items in other parts of the store, and then go to the lunch counter. They would sit there quietly, with dignity and with a firm insistence on their right to be served. For these students the central issue was not the hamburgers or Cokes. The issues were justice, human dignity, fairness, equality, and freedom. They were all driven by the desire to reach the fundamental goal: "Jim Crow Must Go."

How did they come to that moment, that decision? How do we explain why four Southern black teenagers decided that they needed to leave the relative security of their campus and go out to confront and challenge an unjust system of racial domination that had been deeply and violently grounded in their region for all of their lives and the lives of their parents and grandparents? There is no one simple answer to that question, but many elements helped to bring them to this pre-sit-in Sunday night statement: "We've been people who talk a lot . . . but . . . its time we take some action now." In their families, in their schools, and in their churches, they knew and had been taught about women and men who had acted for freedom in years before them.

The three young men who had grown up in Greensboro (McNeil came from Wilmington) were fully aware of a strong local tradition of chal-

In Greensboro, students were models of nonviolence as they vowed to sit quietly at the segregated lunch counter until they were served. These students sat all day at the Woolworth's counter and returned the next day.

lenging segregation. They and their parents had been active in the NAACP, and they had heard of blacks who fought to desegregate the local schools. They attended NAACP-sponsored public presentations by black student pioneers of the effort to desegregate Central High in Little Rock. And, of course, they all had as an example the noble actions of Rosa Parks and Martin Luther King, Jr., the best-known public heroes of the successful Montgomery bus boycott. When King spoke in Greensboro in 1959, Ezell Blair, Jr., remembered that his sermon was "so strong" that "I could feel my heart palpitating. It brought tears to my eyes." The young men knew that they could go to jail. Or there could be violence. So it was not surprising that David Richmond later recalled that "all of us were afraid" that Sunday night before their planned action; yet, he added, "We went ahead and did it."

Monday morning, February 1, 1960, was the day they "did it." After their classes were over at A&T, the young men headed down to Woolworth's, tried to look as casual as possible while purchasing items like toothpaste, notebooks, and pencils, and then moved toward the lunch counter. When they sat down and asked clearly for coffee and snacks and were told that they could not be served, they refused to get up from their seats. Like Rosa Parks, they believed that holding their seats was essential to affirming their dignity and their place as citizens. So Blair, their chosen spokesman, responded to the refusal of service with a polite but probing inquiry: "I beg your pardon," he said, "but you just served us [at the other counters], why can't we be served here?"

By that time other customers were noticing the four neatly dressed, quietly determined young black men. The manager asked them to leave, but they refused, still quiet, still polite, perhaps hearing the old spiritual within them: "We shall not be moved." As a matter of fact, not only did they say they would stay until the store closed, but they announced that they would return again the next day, and the days after that, until they were served, until all black people could be served and their humanity duly recognized—at least at that lunch counter. By then, McClain later remembered, "We had the confidence . . . of a Mack truck."

But it was more than confidence. When McClain recalled that first sit-in in an interview more than 20 years later, he reported, "If it's possible to know what it means to have your soul cleansed—I felt pretty clean at that time. I probably felt better on that day than I've ever felt in my life. . . . I felt as though I had gained my manhood, so to speak, and not only gained it, but had developed quite a lot of respect for it." Joseph McNeil recalled similar feelings that day. He said, "I just felt that I had powers within me, a superhuman strength that would come forward."

That afternoon's action concluded when the manager ordered the store closed. By the time the four freshmen returned to the campus, word of their action had streaked through the classrooms, dormitories, dining halls, and gymnasiums. Many of their fellow students soon pledged their determination to return to the lunch counter the next day.

The example set by the freshmen was so powerful that the new excitement could not be confined to one campus or one city. The students at Bennett College, a private, black women's school nearby, heard the news and joined the fight. Within a few days this powerful moral action had also become a challenge to local white undergraduates, starting with students at the elite Women's College of the University of North Carolina, located in Greensboro. Beginning on Thursday, February 4, small groups of them decided to join the demonstration and risk all the protection of their whiteness, to risk their social and family connections, and to reconsider the meaning of democracy, Christianity, and human dignity.

Before the week was over, the relatively low-keyed action of the four sit-in leaders had escalated to unexpected levels. Nineteen students came to Woolworth's on the second day, and more than 80 were present on Wednesday. Now there were more students ready to sit in than there were

seats at Woolworth's lunch counter. So, the nearby S. H. Kress store
became the next target, and by Saturday of that first week hundreds of students from A&T were streaming into the downtown area to participate in
what had become a kind of student crusade. Even members of the A&T
football team—including a quarterback named Jesse Jackson—abandoned
the apolitical, disengaged stance that marked so many college athletes.
They were on the scene when gangs of young white men, waving
Confederate flags, began to harass the black students, attempting to block
their access to the lunch counters. On at least one occasion, members of
the A&T football team, waving small U.S. flags, opened a path through the
threatening white crowd for the sit-in squads. When one of the
Confederate flag-holders shouted to the team members, "Who do you
think you are?" the response was immediate: "We're the Union army!"
Though the tension was high, there was no further physical engagement,
largely because of the nonviolent discipline of the black students.

By the next week the new, youth-led movement had spilled over into
other North Carolina cities, as students in Durham, Winston-Salem,
Charlotte, Chapel Hill, and elsewhere began their own sit-in campaigns. In
Chapel Hill, as in other cities, there were demonstrators with picket signs
on the streets as well as students sitting at the lunch counters. Several of
the Chapel Hill demonstrators carried signs that expressed the message
they wanted all Americans to hear: "We do not picket just because we want
to eat. We can eat at home or walking down the street. We do picket to
protest the lack of dignity and respect shown to us as human beings."

None of this activity had been pre-planned or coordinated. But, as
one Charlotte student put it, the sit-ins provided a "means of expressing
something that had been on our minds for a long time." Speaking for his
generation of activists, Greensboro's Joseph McNeil said, "I guess everybody was pretty well fed up at the same time."

By the middle of February 1960, the nation had begun to discover
that "everybody" really meant *everybody* and not just the North Carolina
students. Within weeks the sit-ins had become a powerful social movement, ranging across the South and evoking imaginative responses of support from many places in the North. Students organized sit-ins at the New
York affiliates of Woolworth's, for example. Longtime black social activist
Bayard Rustin and singer and actor Harry Belafonte helped organize the
Struggle for Freedom in the South, which raised funds to cover legal fees
of arrested sit-in participants. The young medium of television helped to

To occupy their time while they were waiting to be served, students participating in sit-ins did their homework and wrote letters.

spread what people called "sit-in fever" across the South and demanded the nation's attention. But there were also human networks that carried the news. All over the South, adult veterans of the long struggle for justice and equality made phone calls, wrote letters, traveled by car to make sure that others knew what had begun in North Carolina and encouraged them to consider what needed to be done in their own communities.

Of course, the students themselves contacted friends, relatives, and members of their fraternities and sororities on other campuses in other states. Lunch counters were usually the focus of the action, but the students soon turned their attention to other forms of public accommodations as well. They created "wade-ins" at segregated public pools and beaches, "kneel-ins" at churches, "read-ins" at public libraries, and "bowl-ins" and "skate-ins" at segregated recreation centers. Usually, the students combined those nonviolent "direct action" challenges with marches and picketing at local city halls, seeking negotiations, demanding that the white elected officials (usually elected only by whites, because black citizens had been denied access to the vote) take responsibility and take action to change the segregation statutes. The upbeat spirit of the students was clear, but it was also clear that such actions were not festive occasions.

After the initial white surprise at these challenges to the laws and tra-

The nonviolent civil rights campaign in Tallahassee targeted segregated lunch counters and movie theaters.

ditions of segregation, resistance to the student actions became very real. In some places it came in the form of arrests by the local police. In other situations the police stood by as white citizens took affairs in their own hands. Angry, frightened, and determined to maintain their historic positions of domination and control, white people frequently attacked the students. Sometimes sit-in participants were dragged from the lunch-counter stools and beaten. Ketchup was poured on their heads. Lighted cigarettes were pressed into their hair and on their exposed necks and shoulders. Women swung handbags at them, and men and boys used sticks and bats. Consistently, the students refused to allow themselves to be diverted from their central purpose or from their nonviolent stance, and they chose not to strike back at their attackers.

In Atlanta, one of the early targets of the demonstrating black students was the cafeteria in City Hall, where a sign announced, "Public Is Welcome." Julian Bond, a Morehouse College student leader and son of Dr. Horace Mann Bond, an internationally known scholar, led a student contingent into the cafeteria on March 15, 1960. There, they were greeted by the manager, who asked, "What do you want?" When Bond replied, "We want to eat," the manager's response was, "We can't serve you here." Bond then said, "The sign outside says the public is welcome and we're the public and we want to eat." They got their food, but the cashier refused to take their money. Bond and 75 of his companions did not get a meal in the public cafeteria that day but a cell in the nearby city jail. However, when they were bailed out of jail the next day, the group immediately organized themselves and other students in the Atlanta University complex (which included Spelman College, Clark College, Gammon Theological Seminary, Morehouse, and Morris Brown College) into what became known as the Committee on an Appeal for Human Rights. This turned out to be the first step toward its emergence as one of the most important student movement groups in the South. Its eloquent and thoughtful "Appeal for Human Rights" eventually appeared in the *Congressional Record*, the *New York Times*, and publications in many other parts of the world:

> We . . . have joined our hearts, minds, and bodies in the cause of gaining those rights which are inherently ours as members of the human race and as citizens of the United States.
>
> We do not intend to wait placidly for those rights which are already legally and morally ours to be meted out to us one at a time. . . . We want to state clearly and unequivocally that we cannot tolerate, in a nation professing democracy and among people professing Christianity, the discriminatory conditions under which the Negro is living today in Atlanta, Georgia.

In Jackson, Mississippi, four students and a white professor from Tougaloo College encountered a violent mob at a Woolworth's lunch counter. The attackers poured ketchup, mustard, and sugar on them, then dragged them off their stools and beat them. The students did not retaliate, but returned to their stools. Photos of the attack were printed in Newsweek.

During those early sit-ins, Atlanta also produced one of the most
powerful nonverbal expressions of the meaning of the student movement.
It came at a lunch counter where a slim, gentle-looking Spelman College
honors student named Lana Taylor was part of the sit-in contingent.
According to one of her fellow students,

> The manager walked up behind her, said something obscene and grabbed
> her by the shoulders. "Get the hell out of here, nigger." Lana was not
> going. . . . She put her hands under the counter and held. He was rough and
> strong. She just held and I looked down at that moment at her hands. . . .
> brown, strained . . . every muscle holding. All of a sudden he let go and left.
> I thought he knew he could not move that girl—ever.

Lana was acting in the best tradition of Gandhi, who often described the
way of nonviolence as "holding on to the truth, come what may."

Of course, Taylor, Bond, and their companions were also in the best
tradition of Atlanta. People who knew Southern black communities of that
time would have expected Georgia's capital city to produce a significant
student movement. Its six black institutions of higher education, the presence of Martin Luther King, Jr., and the SCLC, the tradition of a distinguished and relatively progressive African-American middle class, and the
existence of a white leadership group that was concerned about maintain-
ing its reputation for moderation (exemplified by Ralph McGill and his
Atlanta Constitution, the best-known Southern newspaper)—all of these
factors could have led contemporary observers to predict that Atlanta students would rise to the occasion of the new movement. They did, but it
was actually the student sit-in leadership of Nashville, Tennessee, that provided the focal point for the emerging student movement.

Capital of the state of Tennessee, self-anointed as "the Athens of the
South," Nashville was home to one of the nation's oldest and best-known
black schools, Fisk University, alma mater of W. E. B. Du Bois, the legendary African-American scholar, journalist, human rights activist, and
Pan-African organizer. In the largely segregated city, black students were
also enrolled at Meharry Medical School, the American Baptist Theological
Seminary, and Tennessee Agricultural and Industrial College, a large,
all-black state school. But it was one of the first black students at Vanderbilt University who played the central role. James Lawson, son of a
Methodist minister and a strong and devout mother, had originally come to
Nashville from Ohio in 1958 as Southern field secretary for the Fellowship
of Reconciliation. The FOR was a mostly white organization of religious
pacifists that had long been involved in a quiet, search for nonviolent

methods of fighting for racial justice in America. Lawson first met Martin Luther King, Jr., when King was visiting Oberlin College in Ohio and Lawson was one of its older undergraduates. When King learned about the impressive personal history and Gandhian commitments of the articulate, self-assured, and spiritually grounded young man, he urged Lawson to come South and work with him in the expanding freedom movement.

Lawson, a year older than King, had already explored many aspects of the world of nonviolent action. In 1951, while active in organized Methodist youth work, Lawson had refused to register for the military draft that was then gathering young men for service in the Korean War. Basing his objection to participation in the war on the nonviolent teachings of Jesus, Gandhi, and his own mother, Lawson had been arrested for resisting the draft after he was denied conscientious objector status. He spent more than a year in jail. While in prison he met other black and white men who were refusing military service based on their religious and philosophical commitment to pacifism and nonviolence. Eventually, Lawson was released on parole in the care of the Methodist Board of Overseas Missions, and he spent three years as a Christian fraternal worker in India under the board's auspices. During this time—while teaching and coaching sports in Methodist schools—Lawson was able to explore more deeply his strong interest in Gandhian nonviolent action. He had already decided that he wanted to help create an American version of Gandhi's spiritually based liberation movement when he happened to see the first story about the Montgomery bus boycott in an Indian newspaper. As he read the article, Lawson literally jumped for joy and vowed to deepen his own commitment to work for racial justice and reconciliation in the United States. So King's later invitation was a powerful affirmation of what Jim Lawson had long been preparing for.

Responding to King's challenge, Lawson decided to explore an earlier invitation from the Fellowship of Reconciliation to become its Southern field secretary, possibly based in Nashville. Lawson also accepted an invitation to develop workshops on nonviolence from the Nashville Christian Leadership Conference (NCLC), an affiliate of King's SCLC that was led by the outspoken black Baptist pastor Kelly Miller Smith. Joined by his white FOR colleague and fellow Methodist minister Glenn Smiley, Lawson began his Nashville responsibilities by leading a workshop on nonviolent action for the NCLC in March 1958. By the fall of that year, he had decided to enroll as a student at the Divinity School of Nashville's all-white,

Black churches were the gathering and inspirational points for demonstrations throughout the South. In Tallahassee, demonstrators pause for prayer before beginning their march.

Methodist-affiliated Vanderbilt University. He was soon offering extended versions of his initial workshop, focused now on ways in which Nashville's segregated world of public accommodations could be challenged and changed by well-trained, committed teams of nonviolent volunteers.

By the beginning of 1960 there were some 75 regular participants in Lawson's weekly workshops at First Baptist Church. Some of them had even experimented with sitting in at some of the downtown lunch counters and then leaving when refused service. They set up role-playing situations, anticipating what they would do and say when they encountered the expected violent opposition in words or deeds.

Then the word came from North Carolina. It appeared as if the action they were preparing for in Nashville had actually begun several hundred miles away. That Friday night at their usual meeting time, the regular Nashville participants were overwhelmed by some 500 students and adults who wanted to join the fight. Because Lawson's corps of nonviolent trainees had been getting ready, they quickly decided to sit in at the segregated Nashville outlets of Woolworth's and Kress, and they wanted to begin the next morning, Saturday, February 6. So Lawson and the workshop veterans spent long hours that night helping other students and others to get ready, imposing discipline on the courageous spontaneity that marked so much of the sit-in movement.

The students who became the heart of the Nashville movement included Marion Barry, a Mississippi native who was a graduate student in chemistry at Fisk University (and later became mayor of Washington, D.C.); Diane Nash and Angela Butler, two student leaders from the Fisk campus; and a trio of students from the all-black American Baptist Seminary, James Bevel, John Lewis, and Bernard Lafayette. After two weeks of almost daily sit-ins without arrests, attacks, or lunch-counter service, they began to hear that the police were ready to begin arresting them and that local white troublemakers were prepared to attack them physically. Undeterred, the Nashville students (joined by several white exchange students on their campuses) were determined to continue their campaign.

When the Nashville students went back downtown, at the start of the third week, the jailing, the ridicule, the spit, the fierce attacks were all waiting for them—and eventually the world saw it. Perhaps even more important, the black community began to experience a new level of solidarity. Adults rallied to the side of their children and students. Such solidarity became one of the hallmarks of the sit-in phase of the movement, providing an important source of strength for the ongoing freedom struggle. Thousands of black citizens showed their willingness to come forward with every needed kind of assistance, from bail money, to food for the imprisoned students, to the impassioned offering of long and deep prayers on behalf of their young freedom fighters.

At the same time, there were some black adults who thought the students were too brash, too uncompromising, too dangerously provocative, and these various points of view led to significant tensions. But the college students' spirit of bold, nonviolent defiance was infectious, and its effect on an even younger generation may have been at least as significant as its challenge to the elders. One of Nashville's high school students from those days later recalled that when the sit-ins began, he paid relatively little attention to them, for he was very wrapped up in his private ambition of becoming a famous and wealthy rock star. So even when the college students started marching right past his high school, Cordell Reagon was still "unconscious," as he put it. Then, Reagon said,

Whites countered civil rights protests in Memphis with signs praising the bastions of the white South: Governor Ross Barnett of Mississippi and Governor George Wallace of Alabama.

One day they came by, and just on impulse I got some friends together and said, "Let's go." We weren't committed to the cause or anything. We just wanted to see what they were up to—it looked exciting. And we hated being left out. So, about five or six friends and myself just walked out of school that day. We cut school, and joined onto the tail end of that march.

That day the marching students had a stop to make on their way to the lunch counters, a stop that opened new possibilities for young Cordell Reagon's life. He said,

They were marching to the jail, where Diane Nash, one of the main student leaders in the movement, was being kept. We go down to the jail, and we're all singing. There up in the jail cell we could see Diane. And everyone was shouting and waving. And I'm just looking. There is something amazing—a black woman only a couple of years older than me, up in this cell. There was some spirit, some power there, I had never seen before. Suddenly, I realized that everyone had marched down the street, and I was all alone staring at the cell. I ran down and caught up with the end of the march. But I figured then I better not let these people go. There is some power here that I never experienced before.

Responding to that power, holding on to those people, Reagon eventually moved toward the center of the movement, becoming one of the first full-time field secretaries for the Student Nonviolent Coordinating Committee (SNCC, pronounced "snick"). He was also a member of SNCC's Freedom Singers, carrying the music, the stories, and the action of the movement around the world. There were young people like Cordell Reagon all over the South. Not long after Reagon caught up with the end of the powerful line in Nashville, students in downtown Orangeburg, South Carolina, demonstrated. There, they faced tear gas, high-powered fire hoses, and police beatings. In Tallahassee, Florida, the students from Florida Agricultural and Mechanical College also encountered tear gas and violence, but they met up at the lunch counters with white students from neighboring Florida State University who had pledged to arrive before them and to share their food if the black students were refused service.

Everywhere in the South black students were meeting these mixed realities: harsh resistance, some overly cautious elders, new self-confidence and transformation, the emergence of new, sometimes unexpectedly courageous white allies, the beginning of some desegregation victories, and a fresh sense of themselves and the meaning of their movement. At the same time, in spite of the growing sense of solidarity, other black adults were troubled and frightened by the unprecedented boldness of the student

Freedom Rally

Sponsored by

OKLAHOMA CITY BAPTIST MINISTERS' ASSOCIATION

And Other Civic, Educational and Cultural
Organizations in Oklahoma County

FRIDAY, JULY 29, 1960—7:30 P.M.

Dr. Martin Luther King Jr.

Principal Speaker
With Mass Interdenominational Chorus

CALVARY BAPTIST CHURCH

300 North Walnut Street
Oklahoma City, Okla.

King's rhetorical and inspirational gifts, commitment to non-violent social action, and his clear leadership role made him a popular speaker at mass meetings and conventions across the nation.

action. Too familiar with the world of white violence and intimidation, these adults wondered what harsh reactions the student uprising would bring. What jobs would be lost, what homes and churches bombed, what bank loans canceled, what licenses revoked, which young careers aborted, which lives lost? Because of such understandably adult concerns, the students especially appreciated the consistent support and encouragement from Martin King's pubilc statements.

Indeed, it seemed as if King clearly recognized that these students embodied some of his own best dreams for the future of a nonviolent, mass-based freedom movement. So he offered great encouragement to their activities whenever possible and tried to interpret them to the world. For instance, speaking in Durham, North Carolina, that winter to a group of student activists, their parents, and other supporters, King declared that the sit-in movement was "destined to be one of the glowing epics of our time." This perceptive leader affirmed the importance of the students' actions as no one of his stature had yet done. Recognizing them as a creative new force in the struggle for justice and democracy in the United States, King said, "What is fresh, what is new in your fight is the fact that it was initiated, led and sustained by students. What is new is that American students have come of age. You now take your honored places in the world-wide struggle for freedom."

Then he urged them to move ahead and "fill up the jails." Ever since the days of Gandhi in India, resistance leaders had issued the call to fill up the jails as both a personal and strategic challenge. On the personal level in America, it urged nonviolent warriors to overcome their justifiable fear of dangerous Southern jails as well as the sense of shame that respectable families experienced when their children ended up there. On the strategic level, it was a call to present so many challengers to the legal system that its machinery would be blocked, making it difficult to carry on business as usual.

By the end of the winter of 1960 the mostly black contingent of Southern students was taking King—and their own consciences—seriously;

their sit-ins were reaching into every Southern state except Mississippi, which was too harsh in its resistance; they were filling up at least some of the jails of the region, and their sophisticated political consciousness and courageous action were catching the attention of the nation and the world. In March some of the leaders of the local movements got a much-needed opportunity to meet together for the first time to catch their breath. The occasion was what had originally been an annual conference of mostly white Southern college student activists. The 1960 session at Highlander Folk School in Tennessee reflected the rapidly changing nature of the Southern student leadership scene. Now, more than half of the 85 participants in the Annual Leadership Workshop for College Students were black student sit-in leaders.

Highlander Folk School, established in the 1930s, was run by a white couple, Myles and Zilphia Horton. Highlander's adult education programs, sometimes conducted by an interracial staff, included interracial conferences and workshops to train citizens to work for social change. It was an extraordinary and risky set of activities in the South in those days.

As a result of its nonconformist agenda and its left-wing friends, the school had experienced much harassment and persecution from local and state government authorities. Nevertheless, the Hortons persisted in their work, making Highlander a well-known resource center for labor movement organizers and for Southern freedom movement workers such as Septima Clark of Charleston, E. D. Nixon, Rosa Parks, Martin Luther King, Jr., and Fred Shuttlesworth.

Since 1953 Highlander had held an annual workshop for college student leaders. For the 1960 workshop, the Hortons chose a new, post-Greensboro theme: "The New Generation Fights for Equality." In that retreatlike mountainside setting, leaders from the sit-in movements and their potential white allies shared experiences, exchanged strategies, and recognized fellow pioneers. They considered long-range goals, explored new meanings of nonviolence, and talked about not only surviving but prevailing while in jail.

And there was time for singing, singing, singing—the flooding soulful glue that held everything and everyone together. By now it was obvious that this was to be a singing movement, especially as it developed in Nashville, where James Bevel, Bernard Lafayette, and the young Cordell Reagon had taken their love for rhythm and blues street-corner singing and moved right into the hymns and spirituals of their home churches. They had begun to realize how powerful they felt when they could sing together with people who were their comrades in the freedom struggle. Singing kept them together. Singing made them strong. Singing in jail ("Woke up this morning with my mind stayed on freedom"); singing on the picket line ("We shall not, we shall not be moved"); singing in the churchlike mass meetings ("Over my head, I see Freedom in the air"). Singing was life. And Highlander was the place to sing their songs of life, to create and exchange new stanzas, to keep on singing sometimes until two in the morning.

At Highlander, Zilphia Horton had discovered anew the power of song in social movements. In her work with union organizers, she had heard the old 19th-century African-American religious song "I'll Be Alright," which became "I Will Overcome." Then she heard the song transformed by black women labor organizers in the 1940s who took it to the picket lines of the justice-seeking Food and Tobacco Workers Union in

Martin Luther King, Jr., is greeted with cheers as he addresses an audience of flag-waving Birmingham school children. The children insisted on joining the 1963 protests, and many of them were arrested and jailed as they marched for equal rights and the desegregation of the city.

Charleston, South Carolina, as a great rallying call: "We shall overcome. . . . Oh yes, down in my heart I do believe, we shall overcome some day." Eventually, it became a kind of community anthem at Highlander. Spontaneously developing new verses out of their own sit-in experiences ("We are not afraid; We shall live in peace; Black and White together"), students sang it into the night, feeling the power of the expanding interracial band of sisters and brothers.

The gathering at Highlander was a valuable development in the necessary process of turning a set of semi-spontaneous, creative, youthful challenges into a powerful, sustained, insurgent mass movement that would eventually break the decades-old bondage of legal segregation in the South. Indeed, some adult veterans of the long black struggle for freedom had already begun to plan for a more formal meeting of the sit-in leaders.

Central among the movement veterans was Ella Baker, a native North Carolinian who in the 1920s had dreamed of becoming a medical missionary. Unfortunately, the financial pressures of the Great Depresssion made her medical school dream unattainable. So after graduation from Shaw University, a black Baptist institution in Raleigh, North Carolina, she moved to Harlem. Soon, she became involved in a number of political and economic organizing activities. These included the development of a consumers' cooperative organization and attempts at organizing African-American domestic workers, who badly needed better wages and working conditions. By the beginning of the 1940s, Baker was on the national staff of the NAACP, serving an important and often dangerous role as a roving organizer of NAACP chapters in the hostile South.

Later, when the Montgomery movement began to catch the attention of the world, Baker became part of a small group of New York–based social activists who called themselves "In Friendship." They initially focused their attention on raising funds to assist black and white Southerners who had suffered economic losses because of their freedom movement activities or sympathies. As a result of her work with "In Friendship," Baker met King and was later encouraged by her New York colleagues—including Bayard Rustin—to return to the South and help SCLC as its temporary executive director, operating from its Atlanta office.

A brilliant grass-roots organizer, Baker was also an articulate and outspoken woman with a feminist consciousness far ahead of her time. Baker therefore found it difficult to work effectively in a leadership role in an organization made up of black pastors who were too often accustomed

Ella Baker, a veteran activist, was instrumental in encouraging student protesters to create their own organization, the Student Nonviolent Coordinating Committee (SNCC).

to seeing women only as compliant subordinates. Nevertheless, as a result of her SCLC position, Baker was strategically located when the Southern student sit-in movement erupted. And as soon as she began to grasp what was happening among the young people, she decided to find a way to bring their leaders together, to encourage their development as a decisive new force in the freedom movement.

Later Baker said that she wanted to encourage their interests "not in being leaders as much as in developing leadership among other people." So she convinced administrators at Shaw University that they should host a conference of the sit-in leaders. She convinced Martin Luther King, Jr., and other SCLC leaders that the organization should put up $800 to cover the basic expenses for what was officially called a Southwide Youth Leadership Conference on Nonviolence, to be held April 15–17, 1960, the Easter weekend break.

Baker and King signed a letter of invitation and sent it out to student activists and their allies all over the nation. The letter called the sit-in movement and its accompanying nonviolent actions "tremendously significant developments in the drive for Freedom and Human Dignity in America." (Many of the more active leaders and grass-roots participants in the Southern movement used "freedom" and "human dignity" to describe the goals of their struggle much more often than "civil rights.") Now, according to King and Baker, it was time to come together for an evaluation of the burgeoning movement, "in terms of where do we go from here."

The young student leaders were ready for such a gathering. Responding to letters, phone calls, and other personal contacts, more than 200 students and adult observers made their way to Raleigh. Of these, about 120 came from more than 50 black colleges and high schools in 12 Southern states. They brought with them a rich treasury of experiences and stories—about organizing, about marching, about opposition forces and their weapons, about nonviolent resistance, about jails, about the jokes that made it possible for them to laugh in some of the most perilous situations. And of course they brought their songs of defiance, of empowerment, of hope. ("Ain't gonna let nobody turn me round," "This little light of mine . . . I'm gonna let it shine," and "We Shall Overcome" were three of the favorites, but the meeting in Raleigh was an opportunity to share dozens more that students would carry back to the front lines of the freedom struggle.)

In an opening address to the conference on Friday night, April 15, the eloquent and insightful Baker spoke pointedly to the adults present when she said, "The younger generation is challenging you and me. . . . They are asking us to forget our laziness and doubt and fear, and follow our dedication to the truth to the bitter end." King, who was only 31 years old himself, picked up a similar theme in another address when he declared that the student movement "is also a revolt against the apathy and complacency of adults in the Negro community; against Negroes in the middle class who indulge in buying cars and homes instead of taking on the great cause that will really solve their problems; against those who have become so afraid they have yielded to the system." In the post-Raleigh years, this double-edged role of the young warriors would continue: inspiration *and* tough challenge to the adult community.

Because he was the freedom movement leader best known to the press, King was initially the focus of attention for the small press contingent at Shaw. But in the course of the first evening's speeches, they had to deal with the powerful presences of James Lawson and Ella Baker. Baker was acknowledged by the students as their prime mentor. Lawson, the official coordinator of the conference, and Baker both encouraged the students to think about forming an independent organization of their own. By the time the evening was over, the students had become the center of the weekend.

And they were eager to seize the opportunities presented to them. Well-attended workshops ranged from discussions of nonviolence to the political and economic implications of their crusade. They discussed and debated proposals for future organizational structure and spent much time and energy exploring the moral and strategic significance of refusing bail. Apparently, they had taken King seriously when he had begun the weekend by announcing to the press that "the students have taken the struggle for justice in their own strong hands." For instance, one of the 10 discussion groups that day focused on the role of "white supporters" in the rising movement. From the heart of that discussion a powerful insight emerged, one that would mark the student-led campaigns for several years.

According to the notes kept by one of the participants, the workshop participants declared that "This movement should not be considered one for Negroes but one for people who consider this a movement against injustice. This would include members of all races."

By welcoming idealistic, non-black participants into their struggle, blacks confirmed one of the best self-definitions of the Southern-based freedom movement: freedom for black Americans freed all Americans. This vision was a central reason why so many socially committed whites were attracted to the movement at large and particularly to the politically conscious and religiously motivated nonviolent student workers. It was not surprising to find among the "observers" at Shaw representatives from such groups as the ecumenical National Council of Churches; the Northern-based Congress of Racial Equality (CORE), which fought for integration; the Fellowship of Reconciliation (FOR); and the overwhelmingly white National Students Association, which represented college students.

The conference concluded with the birth of the Student Nonviolent Coordinating Committee. Conferees elected Marion Barry the new ogranization's first chairman. Barry held that post through the fall of 1961, when he returned to graduate school in Nashville. During his brief tenure, he established a tone that characterized the group well into the late 1960s. He professed SNCC's intention of directly and forcefully confronting segregation and injustice, even vowing to go to jail to achieve results.

The nation had seen and felt nothing like this bold commitment, moral fervor, religious zeal, and youthful ardor for a cause since the days of the 19th-century abolitionist movement. In those years, too, young people brought their righteous energy and total concentration to play a central role in the struggle against the institution of American slavery. Now, in the spring of 1960, the great-grandchildren of the slaves were leading a new crusade against the legalized remnants of slavery and white supremacy.

In 1961, integrated groups of Freedom Riders were attacked in Alabama and their buses were burned.

CHAPTER 5

THE ARDUOUS TASK: ROOTING OUT FEAR AND GETTING OUT VOTES

In one of his characteristically insightful essays on the American condition, Ralph Ellison, author of the classic *Invisible Man,* wrote these words: "The business of being an American is an arduous task." In the context of the African-American struggles of the 1960s, this was perhaps an understatement. For what emerged from the Southern freedom struggle by the beginning of the 1960s was the clear recognition that the arduous task for black people would be redefining what it means to be an American. Nowhere was this work of re-creation more evident than in the battles for justice that took place in Alabama, Georgia, and Mississippi in 1961.

In May of that year, CORE organized an interracial group of activists to challenge a Supreme Court order outlawing segregation in bus terminals. Calling themselves Freedom Riders, they set out across the South to see if they could integrate all bus terminal facilities, including lunch counters, waiting rooms, and rest rooms. They began their ride in Washington, D.C., and originally hoped to end it in New Orleans. Where they failed, they hoped to draw attention to the continued racism in the South and the need for federal intervention to protect black rights. All was relatively peaceful until they entered Alabama. But the riders met with violence in almost every city they stopped in throughout that state. In Anniston, for example, mobs actually threw a bomb on the bus and set it on fire.

As a result of international publicity, President John F. Kennedy and Attorney General Robert Kennedy tried to persuade the riders to stop their journey. When they refused, the Kennedys struck a deal with Mississippi officials, allowing them to maintain segregated facilities as long as the Freedom Riders were not harmed. Instead of being attacked, riders in Mississippi were simply arrested. Altogether, at least 328 Freedom Riders served time in Mississippi's jails. Realizing that the negative publicity would not die down and that CORE would continue to challenge segregation, Robert Kennedy asked the Interstate Commerce Commission (ICC) to issue an order banning segregation in terminals that catered to interstate transportation. That September, the ICC complied with the attorney general's request, issuing a statement that all interstate facilities must obey the Supreme Court ruling.

The next battle took place in Albany, Georgia, a city of approximately 60,000 people that was intimately shaped by its agricultural setting and the racial attitudes of its Black Belt location. Bernice Johnson, who later married Cordell Reagon, was one of the most powerful participants in the Albany movement. She was a student at the segregated Albany State College in 1961 when the emerging Southern movement began to take hold in Albany. She later remembered that she and other Albany students had heard about the sit-ins and the Freedom Rides of 1961, which occurred when trained interracial teams decided to ride buses through the South and expose illegal segregation practices. She said, "We belonged to black people. Nationally black people were doing something, and we would say, 'When is it going to happen [here]?'" Before long, she was helping to make it happen there.

As an officer of the Youth Council of the local NAACP, Johnson had been one of the students who marched in 1961 on the college president's house to protest the administration's failure to develop adequate security measures against white intruders from town. Such men regularly harassed students on the campus and more than once sneaked into women's dormitories in an attempt to intimidate and sexually threaten the students.

So Johnson, many of her fellow students, and some of their parents were already preparing to challenge the system when representatives of SNCC appeared in Albany that fall of 1961. Recognizing that it was really not able to coordinate a widely scattered Southern student movement that had already begun to change its character, the fledgling organization had decided to become essentially a committed group of antisegregation organizers. More than a dozen of the core group of SNCC people announced late that spring and summer that they were dropping out of school for a year in order to commit themselves to the struggle for justice, dignity, and hope. It was also during this summer of 1961 that the group decided that it would send out "field secretaries" to do grass-roots organizing, especially educating and preparing potential voters across the South, working for

President John F. Kennedy, like his predecessor, sought to balance civil rights demands against political pressures by encouraging activists to pursue non-confrontational strategies.

SNCC at subsistence wages of $25 to $40 per week, depending on whether they were single or married. It was during that same period that the young freedom workers engaged in a series of very long and piercing debates with each other about whether the organization should continue to commit itself to nonviolent direct action or focus instead on voter registration in the Deep South.

SNCC's ongoing internal debates became so heated at times during that summer of 1961 that the new organization seemed in danger of breaking apart. One of the major forces pushing the organization to focus on voter registration was President John F. Kennedy and his brother, Robert, the U.S. attorney general. They were urging the Southern freedom movement organizations to take their primary action "out of the street" and focus on what the Kennedy brothers assumed would be a less volatile—and therefore less internationally embarrassing—action of registering black voters. As a part of their proposal, the Kennedys promised to round up foundation funds for the voter registration campaigns and to assure federal protection for its participants. Of course, not only were the Kennedys and their friends hoping to get the movement off the front pages of the world's newspapers, but they expected that the vast majority of any new black registered voters would be ready to cast their votes for the Democratic party—especially if that party appeared to be committed to securing their rights.

Many of SNCC's young people brought a high level of moral sensitivity and political savvy to their work. So it was not surprising that in the course of the long meetings, many of them thought they saw political and financial bribery at work in the Kennedys' offers. For some who had recently come out of the terror of the Freedom Rides and the resultant rigors of Mississippi's Parchman Penitentiary, any call to turn away from such direct action was a call to betray their history. So the internal battle was a hard one, and it was only the wisdom of their trusted mentor, Ella Baker, that finally led the students to the decision that avoided a split. The "band of brothers," as they had begun to call themselves—reflecting both the sexism of the time and the deep love and respect these young men and women shared for each other—decided to set up a "direct action" project and a "voter registration" project within the one organization.

That fall two SNCC voter registration organizers headed into Southwest Georgia, considered by black people to be a region of the state most resistant to such activities. SNCC had already begun to develop its risky practice of choosing the most difficult and dangerous places to start its projects, working on the assumption that once the "hardest nuts" in a state were cracked, it would be possible to assure local people and their own members that they could take on anything else. But "Terrible" Terrell County—SNCC's chosen starting point—proved to be too much at first. It was a place too filled with the fear and the bloody memories of its black people and the brutality of its white citizens to be ready for the voter registration action that Charles Sherrod and Cordell Reagon had in mind. Sherrod was a seminary student from Virginia who had left school to join SNCC's crusade. His 18-year-old companion was the same Cordell Reagon who had been drawn out of his Nashville classroom the previous year by the sheer power of that city's student movement.

So they turned toward Albany, the largest town in the area. Because an order of the Interstate Commerce Commission banning segregation in all interstate travel facilities (notably, bus terminals and train stations) was scheduled to take effect on November 1, 1961, Sherrod and Reagon decided that they should encourage the local black young people of Albany to test the ICC mandate. In this way they could take "direct action."

As the first SNCC people on the scene in Albany, Sherrod and Reagon had to improvise in organizing the black people there. The two men also had to figure out a way to reach the most receptive young people in the African-American community without seeming to compete with the local NAACP chapter and its own Youth Council. Reagon later remembered how they went about the task of getting people their own age involved: "We slept in abandoned cars, and eventually we started going out on the college campus. We would sit in the student union building on the college campus all day long, drinking soda, talking with the students, trying to convince them to test the public accommodations at the bus station."

SNCC organizers like Reagon and Sherrod were key in bringing teenagers into the center of the freedom movement of the 1960s. Their methods were basic and direct. According to Reagon,

> We spent many days in the playgrounds at high schools. We went to football games, and went to programs at the school. We talked to the students. We'd go to their homes. You know, we'd hang out and play ball with 'em, whatever . . . we did a little bit of everything. We became a part of that community. And after people got over their initial fears of us, I mean we were taken in as sons of the community.

102

The SNCC workers and their young student compatriots appeared at the Trailways bus terminal in Albany on November 1, 1961, ready to test the new federal desegregation mandate. On that same day, other bus terminals in scores of Southern and border cities were tested in a CORE-inspired follow-up to the Freedom Rides. The Albany action that day marked the beginning of a rising tide of student-led nonviolent confrontations with the city's police force as blacks met an incoming train carrying an interracial group of Freedom Riders. Although the passengers disembarked without incident, the confrontation inspired the formation of a coalition among SNCC, the local NAACP, a local ministers group, and others, which became known as the Albany Movement.

Sherrod and Reagon were the SNCC representatives. By now the two young men were conducting their own version of the direct-action training workshops that Reagon had attended in Nashville. As in Nashville, young people were the central actors in the drama that was building. With the help of SNCC, they talked about directly challenging segregation, including, when appropriate, Chief Laurie Pritchett's police force.

Albany's young people staged their challenge to the bus system on Wednesday, November 22, the day before Thanksgiving. Normally, on that day, Albany State's many out-of-town students would file dutifully into the "colored" side of the bus and train terminals to travel home for the holiday break. This time, even before the crowd of college students arrived, three high school students from the SNCC-revived NAACP Youth Council walked into the white side of the bus terminal. When the police ordered them to move, they refused—and were arrested. Although they were quickly bailed out by the head of the local NAACP branch—who was not happy about the path on which Reagon and Sherrod were leading his youth—their audacious action was like the first crack in a dam.

Before long the college students arrived at the terminal. They had heard about the arrest of the high school students, and their college dean was there to try to make sure his students were not carried away by their new sense of duty. He directed them to the "colored" side. Nevertheless, two Albany State students from the SNCC workshop, Bertha Gober and Blanton Hall, refused. A detective informed them that their presence in the white ticket line was creating a disturbance, and when Gober and Hall did not leave, they were arrested. Like Rosa Parks six years before, they knew what they had to do. So did Chief Pritchett, and he threw the two students in jail.

Their presence in Albany's dirty jail over the holiday became the magnet that drew the larger black community of the city together. Not only did people bring Gober and Hall a steady stream of Thanksgiving dinners, but the Albany Movement leaders took the arrests, along with those of the high school students, as a sign that they had to join their children in the challenge to the old ways. The city and its youth-inspired movement caught the attention of the national press, and the Albany Movement held its first Montgomery-like mass meeting on the Saturday evening after Thanksgiving, November 25. By then Gober and Hall had been bailed out of jail, but they had also been suspended from college by their easily intimidated administrators, a decision that only solidified black community support for the students. At the Saturday night mass meeting, all the religious fervor of Albany's black people was poured into the songs that the students had brought out of their workshops and their jail cells and transformed for the occasion. When they sang "Ain't gonna let nobody turn me round," it became "Ain't gonna let Chief Pritchett turn me round." "This little light of mine" thundered out, and the singers moved past a gentle Sunday School statement to a bold and positive declaration that "I've got the light of freedom, [and] I'm gonna let it shine. . . . Everywhere I go" they pledged, "I'm gonna let it shine." New words poured out: "All in the jailhouse, I'm gonna let it shine." The Albany Singers, including Bernice Johnson, were principally responsible for defining the music of the civil rights movement. Later, Johnson founded the women's singing group Sweet Honey in the Rock.

Beyond the songs that night, the people heard a word from the jailhouse, a word spoken in the soft voice of Bertha Gober. Stretching to stand tall in the gathering, the petite Gober explained her decision in the bus terminal to the people. Then she told them about what it meant to be in jail for the cause of freedom. She said, "I felt as a human being. . . . I had a right to use all facilities [at the terminal]. I felt it was necessary to show the people that human dignity must be obtained even if through suffering or maltreatment. . . . I'd do it again anytime." She added, "After spending those two nights in jail for a worthy cause, . . . I have gained a feeling of decency and self-respect, a feeling of cleanliness that even the dirtiest walls of Albany's jail nor the actions of my institution cannot take away from me."

By now the people at the meeting were ready to do more than sing and listen to testimonies. They were prepared to march on City Hall to demand enforcement of federal law, the reinstatement of the Albany State students, and the end of segregation. Over the next two weeks, at least three groups marched, praying for and demanding change, and when they did, they were arrested in scores. The steady rising of their inspired people actually surprised the leaders of the Albany Movement, among them movement president Dr. William Anderson, a local osteopath, and vice president Slater King, a local realtor. They were not prepared for a situation in which nearly a thousand people, including parents and breadwinners, were at one point stranded in jail with no bail money available and no significant response to their call for desegregation of public transportation facilities.

It was at this point that some of the leadership, especially Anderson, decided that they needed the help of Martin Luther King, Jr. Anderson was a college friend of Ralph Abernathy and a fraternity brother of King. He decided to use these connections to bring in the best-known hero of the Southern movement to see if his presence could bring greater national attention to their struggle, and thereby shake the resistance of the white establishment.

This determination to call in King and SCLC widened divisions that were already present in the Albany Movement leadership. For instance, additional SNCC forces had come in to help Sherrod and Reagon as the work expanded, and SNCC adamantly opposed calling in King and SCLC. Its leaders argued that the media attention King would attract might well suffocate the creative development of a local grass-roots leadership and that they could become too dependent on the star of the freedom struggle.

After black teenagers had gathered at the Albany public library to sing and pray as part of a protest, white police officers quickly moved in and arrested them.

Nevertheless, King, Abernathy, and some of their SCLC staff arrived in Albany for a December 16 mass meeting that they understood to be a one-night inspirational event. But at the meeting Anderson publicly maneuvered King into leading a march the next day. As a result, King and his organization became enmeshed in a very difficult situation.

Increasingly, Albany attracted black and white allies from across the nation. Religious communities were especially attracted to the strong church component of the movement's mass meetings, marches, and mass jailing. But Albany's black leaders, now joined by King and the SCLC, were working for something that had never been attempted in the South before. They had moved beyond the immediate confrontational settings of the bus and train terminals and were pressing for the desegregation of the entire city, beginning with its municipally owned public accommodations and its local bus lines. Such a development was a necessary and inevitable step in the burgeoning Southern struggle, but no one knew how to organize for it or to develop a citywide strategy. Much later, Charles Sherrod admitted, "We didn't know what we were doing. We'd never done it before."

The movement's task was complicated by the fact that Laurie Pritchett, the chief of police, was not a volatile loose cannon like some of his counterparts in other Southern communities. Instead, Pritchett was very concerned about public relations and insisted that his officers rein in their tendencies toward violent treatment of the black community, especially when they were under the scrutiny of the mass media. This strategy was meant to deprive the movement of emotional rallying points and to deprive an already recalcitrant federal government of any reasons for entering the Albany situation. Partly because of Pritchett's strategy, partly because of divisions within the Albany Movement, partly because of the unprecedented demands that they were pressing on the segregated city, and partly because of their own inexperience with such a setting, King, SNCC, and the Albany Movement leaders were unable to reach their immediate goals of achieving the desegregation of public facilities, such as libraries, swimming pools, and courthouses. They could not get the city fathers to expose the racist violence that had kept the black community down for so long. Pritchett undermined the very basis of nonviolent passive resistance by refusing to respond with violence. There were no dramatic images of activists being attacked or beaten by mobs. Instead, they were peacefully arrested for breaking the law.

Pritchett's strategy of limiting publicity was best illustrated by his response to one of three Albany jailings of Martin Luther King, Jr., and his fellow SCLC leader, the Reverend Ralph Abernathy. After each arrest for their role in the Albany demonstrations, they chose to remain in jail in order to make a point of their sacrifice and to heighten national outrage over the situation in Albany. After the first arrest, they were released on bail after negotiations with city officials. It was a hoax. King would later return to jail when he refused to pay bail on the earlier charges. But after one day in jail, Pritchett released them, claiming that a "well-dressed" black man had bailed them out. When King and Abernathy protested their release, Pritchett ignored their pleas and insisted that they leave.

The Albany struggle was transforming the lives of many of its participants. A quarter of a century later, Bernice Johnson Reagon recalled what the movement and its singing had brought to her life:

> The voice I have now, I got the first time I sang in a movement meeting, after I got out of jail. The voice I have now I got that night and I'd never heard it before in my life. At that meeting, they did what they usually do. They said, "Bernice, would you lead us in a song?" And I did the same first song, "Over My Head I See Freedom in the Air," but I'd never heard that voice before. I had never been that me before, And once I became that me, I have never let that me go.

There was no victorious breakthrough in Albany for several reasons. The Kennedy administration agreed not to intervene directly, either to enforce the ICC ruling or to protect the civil rights activists, as long as the Albany authorities could keep the peace. Pritchett succeeded not only in keeping the peace and reducing publicity, but in defeating the movement there. By the end of 1962, a year after the Albany campaign started, SCLC called the campaign off, although SNCC activists remained in Albany for another six years. Segregation was still firmly in place, and only a handful of African Americans could vote.

Nevertheless, even in failure, the movement gained a new vision, a new voice. Partly by accident it had chosen to try to challenge the segregation patterns of an entire Southern city. This was the first time in the post-Montgomery years of the freedom movement that young people and their elders had marched and gone to jail together, had together shaped an organization to challenge segregation. As important, the movement had discovered its capacity to take on more than a boycott, or a sit-in, or a voter registration project. It had learned something through failure. These lessons would be important when King and the forces of SCLC eventually responded to the invitation from their fearless comrade, Fred Shuttlesworth, and moved in the spring of 1963 toward Birmingham, perhaps the toughest, most terrifying city in America in which to stage a fight for desegregation.

The road to Birmingham was not the only path that the Southern movement took in those years following the sit-ins and the Freedom Rides.

Even while the Albany Movement was at its height, a small but steady
stream of SNCC's voter registration workers arrived in the counties that
Sherrod and Reagon had originally targeted. As the Albany campaign
slowed down in 1962, Sherrod himself went back into the nearby rural
areas to lead the work on the voter registration project in Baker, Terrell,
Lee, and Dougherty counties.

Although it rarely received the same kind of media attention as the
dramatic public confrontation of marches, demonstrations, and sit-ins, this
sort of tedious, demanding, unglamorous, and dangerous day-to-day work
of voter registration was an essential step in providing blacks with the tools,
and the power, to transform the nation.

When SNCC members went into places like "Terrible" Terrell
County and "Bad" Baker County, they knew that the people there were
scared. They were afraid of being beaten or killed or of losing their jobs or
their homes if they dared to try to register to vote. Nevertheless, the
SNCC workers found local people already overcoming their fears.

The work of these voter registration campaigners began simply: they
made themselves known in the local black community—where they were
often identified as "Freedom Riders." They visited homes, churches,
schools, individuals, and families, and they sought out black community
leaders. Part of their work was searching for places to live and eat. (Of
course, most rural Southern communities had no motels in the early 1960s,
and those that existed were closed to black people and to whites who
appeared to be "troublemakers." Besides, the subsistence pay that SNCC
provided could not handle even the most modest motel rates.) Usually
through subterfuges, they had to find a place where they could set up the
most rudimentary office, often called a Freedom House, perhaps get a
phone installed, and begin meeting to work out their strategy.

Central to their strategy was always the work of "canvassing." Moving
on foot, on bicycles, in cars, on mules, the young men and women went
from house to house, often at night, asking if people were registered or if
they wanted to register, telling them about the benefits of voting, letting
them know that classes were being set up to help people deal with the
intentionally complicated registration process, and calming their fears.

In the long, hard work of breaking the power of fear in places like
Terrell County, one of the most important examples was set by the freedom
workers in jail. They all experienced jail, often many times. These were
places of terror for most of the local black community. In these dank, often

*In Mississippi, the
movement focused on
voter registration
drives, seeking to
give blacks a voice in
the government that
had excluded them.
This woman proudly
displays her voter
registration card.*

filthy settings, the county sheriffs and deputies held almost total, devastating, and sometimes sadistic power. Almost every black person in the county knew someone who had been beaten nearly lifeless in jail, and it was part of the local lore that men too often went into jail and never came out alive. The SNCC workers in Southwest Georgia knew something of this history and realized it was part of the terror tactics that white supremacists used to maintain their power over black people. So, early in Sherrod's time in the area, when he was taken to Sheriff Z. T. "Zeke" Mathews's jail with other freedom movement demonstrators, a confrontation was both inevitable and necessary. Outside the jail, as they were being taken into the once dreaded place, Sherrod was leading freedom songs and prayers. Sheriff Mathews, who was escorting them into the jail, gruffly announced, "There'll be no damn singin' and no damn prayin' in *my* jail." Then the sheriff added, "I don't want to hear nothin' about freedom!" Sherrod immediately spoke up: "We may be in jail, but we're still human beings and still Christians." The Sheriff punched him in the face. Then Mathews took the freedom worker into his office where another officer hit him again, cracking open his lip. With his mouth full of blood, Sherrod was thrown into a cell by himself. But he had already set a powerful example of what it might mean to be a human, a Christian, and a nonviolent fighter for freedom.

Despite the dangers, young people were willing to join the freedom fighters in their perilous and demanding work. Sammy Mahone, a high school junior in Leesburg, Georgia, was one of these local heroes. Early in his work with the project, he went with an elderly black woman to help her with her application for registration. The registrar on duty that day began cursing at Sammy. This so unnerved the applicant that she left without completing her application. Sammy, however, stood his ground and complained to the registrar. The white official raised his fist, and Sammy said, "You mean to tell me you'd hit a kid like me?" The response from the registrar was, "Yeah, cause you got no business here. These people here ain't your concern." The teenager came back with, "I think they're my concern. I'm a citizen and a Negro and I have every right to be here in this building." With that, the registrar had had enough of Sammy Mahone and walked out, snarling to his young antagonist, "You ain't nothing."

The atmosphere of confrontation and overcoming fear became most evident in a meeting in Sasser, a country town in Terrell County. On Monday night, July 25, 1962, Sherrod, some of his interracial SNCC comrades, and several of the local black leaders and participants were carrying on their weekly voter registration meeting at Mount Olive Baptist Church. There were some 30 or 35 people in the building. Attendance was lower than usual partly because of a threat from whites that the gathering would be broken up.

But the meeting went on, likely encouraged by the presence of three national newspaper reporters who had also heard about the threat. The session began, as usual, with a hymn, a prayer, and a Bible reading, the necessary ingredients for starting a meeting anywhere in the black South. Sherrod was in charge of this part of the meeting. The anxiety level was higher than usual that night, but the SNCC organizer kept his voice even and calm as he opened the session. They sang, "Pass me not/O gentle Savior," and then repeated the Lord's Prayer together. Sherrod led them in repeating the Twenty-third Psalm, slowing down on the words, "Yea, though I walk through the valley of the shadow of death, I will fear no evil." Just then they heard the sound of car doors slamming in the driveway.

Sherrod had begun to read one of his favorite passages from the New Testament. When he heard the car doors, he said quietly, firmly, "They are standing just outside now. If they come in I'm going to read this over again." He read from Romans 8:31, "If God be for us, then who can be against us?" At that point about 15 white men from Sasser walked in, including one in a deputy sheriff's uniform, along with Sheriff Mathews, in plain clothes. They lined up against the wall in the back of the church while Sherrod completed the reading. Then, without missing a beat, the young freedom minister began to pray: "Into thy hand do we commend our minds and souls and our lives every day. . . . We've been abused so long. . . . We've been down so long." The "Amens" and "Uh-huhs" of the people had begun to roll into place between his phrases, and they came again when Sherrod went on. "All we want," he said, "is for our white brothers to understand that Thou who made us, made us all. . . . And in Thy sight we are all one." Sheriff Mathews had bowed his head and closed his eyes.

Sherrod continued, "We aren't praying for safety from the storms of life. We're praying for strength to go through the storms of life. And, oh Lord, we pray for Love. . . . The Love that allows us to stand up to our adversaries and love them despite the evil they do to us." Again, there were many "Amens," but the white men against the back wall were silent.

Sherrod led the strangely mixed congregation in the Lord's Prayer, and then someone began singing, "We are climbing Jacob's ladder." Soon after the song began, the men in the back filed out. At the end of the song

Sheriff Mathews, accompanied by two of his deputies and the sheriff of neighboring Sumter County, walked back in. One deputy now had a large revolver holstered on his belt, and the other one was brandishing a two-foot-long flashlight, a familiar weapon.

By this time, Lucius Holloway, the local chairman of the voter registration drive, had begun to lead the meeting, and he called out to the lawmen,

Poll taxes, literacy tests, and citizenship exams were routinely used to keep blacks away from the polls in the South.

"Everybody is welcome. This is a voter registration meeting." Sheriff Mathews responded:

> We are a little fed up with this registering business. Niggers down here have been happy for a hundred years, and now this has started. We want our colored people to live like they've been living. There never was any trouble before all this started. It's caused great dislike between colored and white.

Then the deputies began taking the names of everyone present, and they told the local black people that they did not need the outsiders from SNCC in order to register. They also issued ominous threats about what could happen to blacks after their outsider allies left the area. In the midst of the lawmen's performance, someone began humming "We Shall Overcome." Others picked up the song. The lawmen retreated to the back of the church and the people continued their meeting, giving reports of registration attempts, testimonies of beatings, and statements of hope.

At the end of the meeting, they gathered in a circle at the church door to sing "We are not afraid." That night there was no violence—except to the tires of one of the reporters' cars. But several nights later, the little church was burned to the ground. Eventually, most of the SNCC workers and community leaders who were at the meeting found themselves thrown in jail, and beaten, as usual. Still, the organizing and overcoming continued in Terrell County and elsewhere in the Deep South.

In these settings it had usually been so long since black people had voted that many local black people did not even know that the nation's laws guaranteed them that right. Voting and politics generally were considered "white folks' business," and there were terrible memories that reminded them of what could happen to blacks who tried to participate in that business. In addition to the physical terror that stood between African Americans and the ballot box, everyone knew of the economic intimidation that was often used against them, sometimes forcing them off the land they were farming as sharecroppers, putting them out of the miserable shacks they lived in, making it impossible to get jobs with local employers—ultimately forcing them to leave the area. These were the settings that had produced black registered voting percentages of 0 to 5 percent in many places where black people made up more than 50 percent of the population.

But in every such setting, there were always people willing to work for a new day. That was certainly what Bob Moses found when he went into Mississippi. Moses had been working in Atlanta as a volunteer in the SNCC office staff in the summer of 1960. He was sent to Alabama and Mississippi that summer to recruit participants for the next SNCC organizing conference, scheduled for the fall. In preparation for the trip, Ella Baker supplied Moses with the names of people she had worked with during her days as an NAACP organizer in the South.

One such person was Amzie Moore, president of the local, somewhat bedraggled NAACP chapter in Cleveland, Mississippi. When Moses met Moore, the 49-year-old Mississippi movement veteran was farming part-time, working a few hours each day in the local post office, and running his own gas station. Because Moore had insisted on trying to develop a voter registration campaign in Cleveland in the mid-1950s, and because he refused to put up the legally required "colored" and "white" signs in his station, he had almost lost his business and his life. But he was still there when Moses arrived, looking for recruits for SNCC.

The sturdily built, straight-talking Amzie Moore was old enough to be Bob Moses' father, and something of that character developed almost immediately in their relationship. After his first few days with Moore, Moses wrote back to a SNCC comrade in Atlanta: "Amzie is the best I've met yet. . . . He lives like a brick in a brick house, dug into this country like a tree beside the water." He added, "I would . . . contact him frequently." In the course of those contacts the recruiter was recruited, and the future of Mississippi—and the nation—began to be transformed.

Moore convinced Moses that what Mississippi needed more than a group of young SNCC-like recruits going off to Atlanta was a band of SNCC's arduous freedom workers coming to Mississippi to create a major voter registration campaign, starting right there in Cleveland. Moses said he would take the message back to Atlanta. But Moses promised that regardless of what SNCC formally decided, he would personally return to Cleveland the following summer. When Moses returned South in the summer of 1961, much had changed throughout the nation. Most important among the changes was the influence of the Freedom Rides and the hope they inspired. And in Mississippi itself, Medgar Evers, the head of that state's NAACP organization, was openly calling for the city government of Jackson, the capital city, to desegregate public facilities.

But the time was still not quite right for a voter registration campaign in Moore's Delta area. White reaction to black assertiveness was swift and violently brutal, federal protection could not be assured, and many blacks questioned the wisdom of "stirring up trouble." Instead, some local NAACP leaders in Southwest Mississippi had heard about the possibility of a SNCC team coming to the state to work on voter registration, and they asked their friend Moore to put them in touch with Moses. As a result, SNCC's voter education wing began its Mississippi development in a small town called McComb, near another town named Liberty. Courageous older NAACP veterans from the area, like C. C. Bryant, E. W. Steptoe, and Webb Owens helped to open the way for Moses, who was soon joined by two former Freedom Riders, John Hardy and Reginald Robinson.

The SNCC forces started in the usual way. With the help of the committed older men and women in the town, they began to introduce themselves to other local leaders and soon sought out the young people as well. Many of the teenage group were fascinated by the fact that these activists had come to their town, and they were ready for any kind of exciting direct action. Their elders, however, knew that people in their area had been beaten, killed, or driven out of town for trying to register to vote. So when Moses and his team began to set up a "school" to help people prepare for the intimidating moment when they might face a hostile registrar, the response was slow. Moses made it a practice never to pressure local people to register, because he knew—and they also knew—that he was asking them to risk their lives, a decision that they had to make themselves.

But when the first group of three local volunteers—an older man and two middle-aged women—were finally ready, it was Moses whose life was most at risk. After helping his frightened candidates break their silence as they faced the registrar, Moses was attacked on the main street of McComb by a man who was the sheriff's cousin. He split Moses's scalp with the heavy handle of a hunting knife. About a week later Moses felt a different kind of pain when he had to identify the body of Herbert Lee, a black farmer who had risked his life to volunteer as a driver for the SNCC voter registration team. Because of his Movement association, Lee had been shot to death in daylight by a white segregationist—a Mississippi state legislator.

Meanwhile in McComb, the committed high school students were too young to register and too impatient to wait. They wanted to enter the freedom struggle more directly than by teaching older people to read the registration materials. By now, SNCC people from the "direct action" contingent—like Marion Barry and Diane Nash—had also begun to gather in McComb, and they were leading workshops for the teenagers on nonviolent direct action. As soon as they could, the students put their training into action with a sit-in at a local lunch counter, the first in that part of Mississippi, an action that SNCC had not planned for. The sit-in squad was put in jail, and some of them were suspended from school. That led to a student-organized walkout from their school and a march to City Hall.

Sensing that the teenagers were moving into a dangerous action that they could not handle, Moses and some of his coworkers decided to march with them. The youngsters decided that they wanted to pray on the steps of City Hall. The police thought prayers belonged only in churches or homes, and they began to arrest the young people. The students were repeating the Lord's Prayer, and each time one was interrupted and arrested, another walked up the steps to continue the prayer. Finally, the police arrested more than 100 young people and took them to jail. By then the spectacle had attracted a crowd of curious and angry white people.

Moses and his two SNCC companions offered a striking testimony to the spirit of SNCC. One of them was Charles "Chuck" McDew, an Ohio-born black college student who became a sit-in leader at South Carolina State College in Orangeburg. The other was Bob Zellner, the organization's first full-time field secretary assigned to recruiting white students. A native of Alabama, Zellner was the son of a white Southern Methodist minister, and he went to McComb instead of traveling to white campuses because he wanted to know what SNCC was actually doing in order to be an effective recruiter for the cause.

However, the white people of McComb wanted to know what *he* was doing there in the midst of the black troublemakers. Here, and in many future situations, Zellner was considered "a traitor to the white race." So as he came down the City Hall steps on his way to jail, several men rushed to attack him. There were many beatings and jailings in McComb that fall. At

Federal marshals protected James Meredith, the University of Mississippi's first black student, during the fall of 1962. Whites responded to his admission with riots on the Ole Miss campus, resulting in the deaths of two people.

one point, all but one of the SNCC organizers were in jail. But it was the death of Herbert Lee that haunted people more than anything else. Despite the harsh white resistance that had forced the adults of McComb to temporarily slow down their attempts at voter registration, leading to SNCC's temporary withdrawal, still no one could miss the tremors of change throughout the state.

In 1962, the most spectacular tremor in Mississippi was the decision of black Air Force veteran James Meredith, with the support of the NAACP, to apply for admission to Ole Miss. Few institutions were considered more quintessentially white Mississippian, more worthy of defense against the black challenge than the University of Mississippi at Oxford. When Meredith first tried to enroll in the university, Governor Ross Barnett barred him from admission, a power that a federal court ruled Barnett did not possess. Barnett then encouraged white people in the state to believe that their active, armed resistance—even to a court-ordered change—could halt desegregation.

So by the end of September 1962, when it was time for Meredith to appear on campus to register for his first classes, thousands of white Mississippians—both students and others—believed that they could physically guard the university against the newly defined black presence that Meredith represented. One state legislator pledged to persevere in mounting physical resistance to the quiet black pioneer, "regardless of the cost in time, effort, money, and in human lives." This was the spirit that led students and their segregationist allies to riot against the federal marshals who had slipped Meredith onto the campus the Sunday afternoon before registration. The rioters hurled rocks, bricks, lead pipes, and tear gas at the marshals, and finally even shot at them in a one-sided battle in which the marshals were ordered not to return the fire. In the course of the uproar, a foreign reporter and a local white worker were shot and killed, and some 350 others, mostly marshals, were wounded. The Kennedys had been trying to negotiate their way to a settlement with Barnett that would not require them to send in federal troops to protect Meredith's rights. However, in the end, the Kennedys decided they had to send in the troops.

Though late, this federal intervention finally ended the white resistance.

As the mounting conflict was seen on television around the world, Meredith waited calmly in his room for the sounds of guns, tear gas canisters, rebel yells, and threatening anti-black chants to die down outside. The next day, James Meredith finally registered as the first black student at Ole Miss and became a powerful symbol to the black people of the nation. One of that state's movement leaders later wrote,

> Almost every black in Mississippi knew that James Meredith was in the University of Mississippi, that Ross Barnett and the Citizens' Council had lost a major round, that the federal government would, in some instances . . . constructively involve itself all the way, even down in Mississippi. For the first time in their lives, Mississippi blacks had seen a very tangible civil rights victory for one of their own. . . . There was a new interest in the battle against segregation and discrimination, especially among youth.

As the SNCC workers reflected on their experiences in southwest Georgia and southwest Mississippi, they moved to the northwest area of Mississippi, known as the Delta. They stopped in Jackson to work out the details of a new coalition. Now they would coordinate their work with the activities of the NAACP, SCLC, and CORE, and together they formed the Council of Federated Organizations (COFO). This coalition was largely Bob Moses' idea, and it served as an important pipeline for the funds that supported registration work.

Ultimately, this united front was important for the morale of Mississippi's black people, providing them with a sense of the joint strength that was needed to break open the "closed society" of their state. Nevertheless, the essential energies and people power of the next stages of the COFO campaign came from SNCC, which was the heart of COFO. SNCC realized that the dangerous and essentially underground work of registering blacks had to become more visible to the world, not only to provide protection and build morale but also to prod the federal government into action.

From the spring of 1962 to the fall of 1963 the Mississippi voting rights work was focused on the Delta region. It was known as one of the most terror-filled sections of a violence-prone state. Partly because of this reputation, partly because this was the area where Amzie Moore lived, Bob Moses, as the new COFO program director, took his voter registration forces there, working to make Moore's old dream come true.

The reality of voter registration in the Delta was harsher than the dreams, however. Once again, the violence was persistent and nerve-wracking. For instance, early in the campaign in the Delta, which was focused on the city of Greenwood, Moses and two companions met the terror. With Randolph Blackwell, visiting from the Voter Education Project, an Atlanta-based funding agency, and Jimmy Travis, a 20-year-old Mississippian who had moved on from the Freedom Rides to SNCC's staff, Moses drove off one night from the Greenwood office with Travis at the wheel. A car followed them and eventually pumped 13 bullets into their vehicle. One bullet entered Travis' neck and stopped just short of his spinal column. Somehow, Blackwell and Moses were not hit. But such danger became the normal setting for the work in Mississippi.

In the Delta, as in every other voter registration campaign in the Black Belt, SNCC and other groups were constantly meeting such men and women as Fannie Lou Hamer of Ruleville, a town not far from Greenwood. The 47-year-old sharecropper with a sixth-grade education went to a mass meeting one night in 1962 and heard James Bevel, the charismatic leader who had emerged from the Nashville student movement, holding forth like an evangelist, calling people to a new life of struggle for freedom. Hamer later said, "Until then I'd never heard of no mass meeting and I didn't know that a Negro could register and vote." But when she found out, she was one of the first volunteers to go to the courthouse the next day.

Hamer knew she was volunteering for danger, and later she said, "I guess if I'd had any sense I'd a-been a little scared, but what was the point of being scared. The only thing they could do to me was kill me and it seemed like they'd been trying to do that a little bit at a time ever since I could remember." From that day on Hamer was at the heart of the movement. Indeed, the next morning, when the old school bus carrying the registration volunteers pulled up to the county courthouse, the folks from Ruleville seemed frozen by fear and no one got off. Not until Fannie Lou Hamer began to sing and to walk, with the limp left from her childhood bout with polio. Limping, singing, and standing as tall as her five-foot, four-inch frame could stretch, she led the group off the bus and into the courthouse, the bastion of white power, prepared to register.

Of course this fight against crippling fear was also one of the greatest challenges faced by the full-time freedom workers, especially those who worked in the roughest places, doing the most dangerous work, for the highest stakes. While in Greenwood, Bob Moses wrote about how to face the long, hard, dangerous times when it was easy to give in to fear:

You dig into yourself and the community and prepare to wage psychological warfare; you combat your own fears about beatings, shootings, and possible mob violence; you stymie by your own physical presence the anxious fear of the Negro community . . . you organize, pound by pound, small bands of people who gradually focus in the eyes of Negroes and whites as people tied up in "that mess"; you create a small striking force capable of moving out when the time comes, which it must, whether we help it or not.

Of course no one could predict how and when the time would come, again and again, in these life-changing campaigns. But for people on the front lines, like Moses, the testing time was always nearby. This was the testimony of one of his coworkers, Marian Wright, a Spelman College graduate who was taking some time from her Yale Law School studies to join the forces of hope in Greenwood. She wrote,

Bob Moses, who led SNCC's voter registration campaigns in Mississippi, speaks to a group of students about the dangers they might face as civil rights volunteers.

I had been with Bob Moses one evening and dogs kept following us down the street. Bob was saying that he wasn't used to dogs, that he wasn't brought up around dogs, and he was really afraid of them. Then came the march, and the dogs growling and the police pushing us back. And there was Bob, refusing to move back, walking, walking towards the dogs.

Neither Moses nor the dogs backed down, and one of the animals tore a piece out of his trousers before his police handler pulled him away. Bob Moses kept walking.

In Greenwood, in 1962 and early 1963, no one knew how long they would have to walk and work, facing dogs, facing death, facing fear. But one thing began to be clear: they were not walking alone. For instance, in response to appeals from SNCC, communities in the North were donating truckloads of food and clothing for desperate Delta families. Dick Gregory, the socially concerned comedian, came to stand in solidarity and mordant humor with the people who continued to walk toward the courthouse and the registrar's office. Folksinger Bob Dylan arrived for his baptism in the work of the movement, sharing his songs and hope.

In the early spring of 1963, many of the full-time SNCC workers took time out from Greenwood's battleground to attend the annual SNCC staff meeting in Atlanta. The organization's full-time staff was now up to 60 people, and they came in from all over the South. Some 350 people attended the April gathering held at one of Atlanta's black theological schools, Gammon Seminary. In typically lengthy sessions, the nonviolent shock troops of the Southern movement and their supporters did much more than present and listen to reports. They came, in SNCC style, to hug and sing and share their woundedness and their humor and to seek release from some of the extraordinary tensions of their dangerous work.

Reflecting later on the session, James Forman, who was the organization's indefatigable executive secretary during those crucial years, summed up the spirit and meaning of the experience: "The meeting was permeated by an intense comradeship, born of sacrifice and suffering and a commitment to the future, and out of a knowledge that our basic strength rested in the energy, love, and warmth of the group. The band of sisters and brothers, in a circle of trust, felt complete at last."

In the midst of a throbbing social movement nothing remained "complete" for long. Even as the SNCC meeting was going on, its companion and slightly elder organization, SCLC, was opening another front of the expanding Southern freedom movement. Responding to repeated invitations from Fred Shuttlesworth, leader of the Birmingham civil rights movement, and determined to learn crucial lessons from the many difficulties and experiments in Albany, in the spring of 1963 Martin Luther King, Jr., and his staff had gone to Birmingham, Alabama.

CHAPTER 6

BIRMINGHAM: THE DAYS BEYOND "FOREVER"

When a bomb planted by white supremacists exploded in the Sixteenth Street Baptist Church in Birmingham, four schoolgirls who were preparing for Sunday services were left dead. Their deaths horrified people of all races and both stunned and galvanized the Southern freedom movement.

When SCLC decided to challenge segregation in Birmingham, Alabama, it was taking on a city with one of the worst records of anti-labor and anti–civil rights violence in the country. Because of its surrounding coal and steel industries, the city had always attracted labor organizing activities. In 1931, the police force established the "Red Squad" to handle communist and other left-wing organizers with force, and from then on Birmingham's law enforcement agencies—with much assistance from private citizens—were infamous for their brutal tactics. During the 1930s, many black and white labor organizers were arrested, kidnapped, beaten, or even killed. And in 1941, Birmingham experienced a wave of police killings and beatings. The best-known incidents involved the deaths of two young black men, O'Dee Henderson and John Jackson. Henderson, who was arrested and jailed for merely arguing with a white man, was found handcuffed and shot the next morning in his jail cell. A few weeks later, Jackson, a metalworker in his early 20s, was shot to death as he lay in the backseat of a police car. He had made the fatal mistake of arguing with the arresting officers in front of a crowd of blacks lined up outside a movie theater.

After World II, blacks often referred to the rigidly segregated city as "Bombingham." The name called attention to the frequent bombings of the homes and churches of those African Americans who dared to take even tentative steps toward the establishment of racial justice. This was the setting in which Birmingham minister Fred Shuttlesworth and his family had been beaten, bombed, attacked, and jailed. Many people agreed with Martin Luther King, Jr., when he said, "As Birmingham goes, so goes the South." Later, when he reflected on the Birmingham campaign, King wrote:

121

We believed that while a campaign in Birmingham would surely be the toughest fight of our civil-rights careers, it could, if successful, break the back of segregation all over the nation. This city had been the country's chief symbol of racial intolerance. A victory there might well set forces in motion to change the entire course of the drive for freedom and justice.

After exploring the situation, SCLC moved into action in Birmingham during the first days of April 1963. This was a period of intense freedom movement activity all across the South, with thousands of demonstrators challenging segregation from Maryland to Louisiana. In Birmingham, SCLC and Shuttlesworth's Alabama Christian Movement for Human Rights (ACMHR) focused on breaking the hold of legalized segregation in all the public facilities, starting with its downtown stores and its municipal facilities, such as city-owned parks, pools, and drinking fountains. They also hoped to open up the police force to black officers. To work out details and to keep the process moving beyond the demonstrations, the black organizations pressed for the establishment of a city-sponsored biracial committee.

In light of Birmingham's history, in the presence of Alabama's new governor, George Wallace, who had loudly declared in his 1963 inaugural address, "Segregation now! Segregation tomorrow! Segregation forever!" this relatively modest set of goals appeared to most white residents to be undesirable, and impossible. Complicating the situation was the fact that the white leadership of Birmingham was deeply divided. When SCLC came on the scene that spring, the city was awaiting a judicial decision concerning a recent, disputed municipal election. The decision would either establish Bull Connor, the police commissioner, as mayor or place in office a more moderate segregationist named Albert Boutwell. At the same time there was a white business community of expanding influence whose members were greatly concerned about their city's image, an image they were trying to refurbish "to look like Atlanta," the liberal showcase city of the region. But in the midst of all of this the Ku Klux Klan and its adherents were still dangerously active, rallying behind their new governor.

For most of April, SCLC's challenge to Birmingham seemed to have a hard time capturing the full energy and interest of local black people or the national press. Even when King and Abernathy were arrested and jailed for marching on Good Friday, April 12, the best of the nightly mass meetings could not produce more than 50 or 60 volunteers for the next morning's demonstrations, which were designed to demand an immediate end to racist employment practices and segregation in public accommodations.

Birmingham police commissioner Bull Connor became a national symbol of white racism when he unleashed attack dogs and fire hoses on peaceful protesters during the 1963 demonstrations.

It was important to note who did show up to march. At the outset of the campaign it was the older people who stepped forward. Eventually, the Birmingham grandchildren would respond to the elders.

While King sat in the isolation cell of Bull Connor's jail, one of his lawyers managed to smuggle in some newspapers. In one of the Birmingham papers King came across a statement signed by a group of local white clergymen who considered themselves friends of black people and open to "moderate" racial change. Expressing concern that the desegregation campaign could play into Bull Connor's hands, they urged King and SCLC to leave Birmingham's future in the hands of its moderate black and white leaders. King seized the opportunity to respond. After a yellow, legal-sized pad was passed on to him, King ended up with a lengthy handwritten document that attempted to lay out the justification for his presence in Birmingham, to express the meaning and purpose of nonviolent direct action, and to provide a statement concerning the role of the churches in the quest for racial justice. However, the single most powerful section of his long letter arose out of his determination to let the white clergymen— and any other readers—know something about what it meant to be a black person in the segregated South, and what it meant to be told by white "friends" and Christian brothers to wait for a more convenient time to protest and challenge the injustice and inhumanity of segregation.

King wrote, "I guess it is easy for those who have never felt the stinging darts of segregation to say, 'Wait.'" Then in the longest sentence he had ever written, or would ever write again, he poured out a statement that was more than a moan or a plea for understanding.

> When you have seen vicious mobs lynch your mothers and fathers at will and drown your sisters and brothers at whim, when you have seen hate-filled policemen curse, kick, brutalize and even kill your black brothers and sisters with impunity, when you see the vast majority of your twenty million Negro brothers smothering in an air-tight cage of poverty in the midst of an affluent society; when you suddenly find your tongue twisted and your speech stammering as you seek to explain to your six-year-old daughter why she can't go to the public amusement park that has just been advertised on television, and see tears welling up in her little eyes when she is told that Funtown is closed to colored children, and see the depressing clouds of inferiority begin to form in her little mental sky, and see her begin to distort her little personality by unconsciously developing a bitterness toward white people; when you have to concoct an answer for a five-year-old son asking in agonizing pathos, 'Daddy, why do white people treat colored people so

mean?'; when you take a cross-country drive and find it necessary to sleep night after night in the uncomfortable corners of your automobile because no motel will accept you; when you are humiliated day in and day out by nagging signs reading "white" and "colored"; when your first name becomes "nigger" and your middle name becomes "boy" (no matter how old you are) and your last name becomes "John," and when your wife and mother are never given the respected title "Mrs."; when you are harried by day and haunted by night by the fact that you are a Negro, living constantly at a tip-toe stance, never quite knowing what to expect next, and plagued with inner fears and outer resentments; when you are forever fighting a degenerating sense of "nobodiness"; then you will understand why we find it difficult to wait.

King's *Letter from Birmingham Jail,* one of the classic statements of the freedom movement, did not begin to reach the outside world until more than a month after it was written. It was published in a number of newspapers and magazines and in book form in 1964 as *Why We Can't Wait.*

Confined in the Birmingham city jail, Martin Luther King, Jr., composed a letter to a group of white clergy of the city, who had urged him to leave the city and wait for a more appropriate time to work for racial justice. His "Letter from Birmingham Jail" described the impact of segregation in graphic detail and was reprinted nationwide.

As the Birmingham demonstrations grew larger and more public, young people were eager to join in. Soon, young people regularly attended the nightly mass meetings and begged their parents to let them join the marches. But the movement leaders debated about encouraging students to miss school for an almost certain rendezvous with prison, or worse. Marchers were attacked by police dogs, shot with high-power water hoses, and beaten with clubs. In that debate the views of SNCC leaders Diane Nash Bevel and her husband, SCLC staff member James Bevel, prevailed. James Bevel, who played a major role as a strategist for the Birmingham protests, argued that since the young people did not carry the burden of their family's economic responsibilities on them, they were free to meet the challenge of going to jail. But the situation soon became more complicated. For as soon as the announcement was made in mass meeting that Thursday, May 2, 1963, would be the day for high school demonstrations, dozens of elementary school children declared their own readiness to march.

Now there was another debate among the leaders. What should be the minimum age for their freedom marchers? They decided that anyone who was old enough to volunteer to become a church member should be old enough to volunteer to become a member of the freedom corps. In that black Baptist-dominated setting, such a decision meant that children as young as six might be on the marching line when Thursday morning came.

That morning Sixteenth Street Baptist Church, the usual meeting place, was filled with hundreds of children. Shuttlesworth offered the morning send-off prayers, and the recently released King told the young people how important they were. They walked out of the church, two-by-two, singing, "Ain' Gonna Let Nobody Turn Me Round." As Bull Connor's policemen soon began to herd them toward paddy wagons and then buses, some of the youngsters darted away and headed downtown. Most of them boarded the jail-bound vehicles still singing, "Ain' gonna let no policemen turn me round . . . Marching on to freedom land." Before the day was over, more than 600 of the children discovered that the way to freedom led directly through Birmingham's jail.

Bull Connor had been caught off-guard on Thursday by the surge of young marchers, moving around the police lines. He did not intend to be upstaged again by a flood of singing black children. So on Friday, May 3, when the young marchers came singing down the steps of Sixteenth Street Church, they saw fire trucks in the park facing the church. Andrew Young, who oversaw SCLC's fledgling voter registration drive and was a chief negotiator in the Birmingham campaign, later described what happened:

Birmingham school children were proud to be taken to jail as participants in the struggle for freedom.

As groups of kids marching past the park headed for downtown, Connor issued the order to the firemen to uncoil their hoses. Police dogs had been seen before, and once again they were brought to the front of the barricades, straining at their leashes. But until now, the fire trucks had remained on the sidelines. Suddenly fire hoses didn't seem like fun anymore, and the kids watched with trepidation as the firehoses were unwound. they kept marching and their voices grew stronger with the comforting tunes of the freedom songs. It never ceased to amaze me, the strength that people drew from the singing of those old songs. . . . Suddenly, Connor ordered the firemen to open the hoses on both the marchers and the large crowd of onlookers who had gathered in the park. The water was so powerful it knocked people down and the line began to break as marchers ran screaming through the park to escape the water. Connor then ordered the police to pursue the terrified kids with angry dogs, and to our horror actually unleashed some of them. The police ran through the park, swinging their billy clubs at marchers, onlookers, and newsmen —anyone in the way. Kelly Ingram Park was exploding with insanity and terror.

As they faced fire hoses with velocity enough to rip bark off trees and to separate brick from mortar, some of the children decided that they would endure the onslaught if they simply held each other's hands.

As the tension escalated, an international audience watched. By now it was clear that the nation's leaders could not continue to avoid direct engagement with the situation in Birmingham and still claim to be "leaders

The Birmingham fire hoses knocked protesters to the ground with enough force to take the bark off trees.

of the free world." The Kennedys, after some initial annoyance with SCLC's timing and methods, let it be known, first privately, then publicly, that they believed a negotiated way should be found through Birmingham's troubles. They sent personal emissaries to the city, especially to urge the business leaders to take responsibility for moving toward desegregation. Robert Kennedy himself made dozens of phone calls to corporate leaders nationwide whose Southern subsidiaries were located in the Birmingham area. He urged them to put pressure on their local people to cooperate with the movement's demands for desegregation.

With the rising pressure of the federal government, negotiations based on the movement's basic demands were finally begun. The negotiations were difficult, but they lasted less than a week. They led to an agreement that was announced on May 7, 1963, about a month after the demonstrations had begun. Under the agreement, an irreversible process of desegregation was begun in public accommodations and municipal facilities. SCLC won its demands for desegregated lunch counters, rest rooms, fitting rooms, and drinking fountains. Downtown store owners agreed to hire African-American clerks. Expanded hiring and promotion of black people was begun throughout the industrial community of Birmingham. All the imprisoned demonstrators were released on bail that was supplied from various local and national sources, and the cases against the released prisoners were soon dismissed. But there was a compromise: SCLC agreed to a timetable of planned stages rather than demanding that these changes take place immediately. It also agreed to the release of arrested demonstrators on bail rather than insist that the charges be dismissed outright.

But it would not be a simple matter to extricate Birmingham from its past. On the evening after the announcement, the Ku Klux Klan leadership bitterly condemned the arrangement at a rally on the edge of the city. Later that night a bomb badly damaged the home of A. D. King, Martin's younger brother, who was an activist pastor in the city and a participant in the movement. Soon, a second bomb exploded at the Gaston Motel, practically demolishing Room 30, the modest suite that King normally used as his headquarters. Fortunately, A. D. King's family was not hurt, Martin King had already left the city, and no one else was injured at the motel. But the bombings drew hundreds of outraged black people into the streets. Without waiting for a request from the new mayor, Albert Boutwell, Governor Wallace sent in state troopers to maintain order. However, the pushing, attacking, cursing troopers seemed intent on provoking the leaderless crowd into violence. In response, black people threw rocks and bottles and set some stores and cars on fire. For a moment it seemed as if a major explosion would blow apart the new agreement. Instead, some of the SCLC and local Birmingham leaders were able to work out a truce between the enraged black people and the brutally aggressive troopers.

The Birmingham campaign, saved from catastrophe, had not only energized the civil rights movement, but it had made the world aware of segregation's ugliness. Television was a critical factor. The new technology enabled millions of viewers to watch with rapt horror as the police attacked the youthful demonstrators. There was no mistaking the haunting scenes of Birmingham police dogs snapping at the legs of children. Nor could even the most casual viewer ignore the fire department's role in the daily confrontations. Armed with water hoses powerful enough to shred clothes and hurl muscular teenagers as if they were leaves blowing in the wind, it was clear that the Southern segregationists would not abandon their cause without dramatic changes in law and social practice.

It became equally clear to the White House that the civil rights activists would not abandon their cause without fundamental changes. An angry encounter between Attorney General Robert Kennedy and African Americans gathered by black writer James Baldwin highlighted the rawness of race relations in the country. Blacks bluntly told Kennedy that they expected more from him and his brother, the President. Robert Kennedy left the room angered by their demands, yet he later reflected that the encounter forever changed his views about race and the race problem in American life. Even the politically pragmatic John Kennedy would under-

A. D. King, the brother of Martin Luther King, Jr., calls for calm following the bombing of his Birmingham home by white terrorists who opposed desegregation.

stand very soon that he could not shrink from the demands for full inclusion. To his credit, President Kennedy tried to get a new civil rights bill through the Congress. The new bill was stronger than all previous ones. It would end discrimination in all interstate transportation, at hotels, and in other public places; it ensured all who had a sixth-grade education the right to vote; and it gave the attorney general the power to cut off government funds to states and communities that contin-

ued to practice racial discrimination. It would be more than a year before Congress passed the Civil Rights Act of 1964. In the meantime, President Kennedy worried that any further demonstrations threatened his ability to secure sufficient bipartisan support for the legislation.

King and others sensed that it was time to bring the strategies of the Southern civil rights movement to the nation's capital. In a private conversation with friends Stanley Levison and Clarence Jones, recorded by an FBI wiretap, King broached the idea of a huge, 100,000-person march on Washington. The FBI had begun to tap King's phone lines after FBI director J. Edgar Hoover convinced Robert Kennedy that Levison, who was white, was a member of the Communist Party and had too much influence over King. Hoover, in fact, had a difficult time believing that blacks had initiated the movement and that it was led by blacks. Unaware that others were listening, King and his friends added other names to the list of possible organizers, including the venerable labor leader A. Philip Randolph, whose earlier threats to march on Washington had led President Franklin D. Roosevelt to issue Executive Order 8802, which banned hiring discrimination at military facilities and government agencies during World War II.

The planning committee brought together representatives from civil rights organizations and the labor movement, interested clergy, and entertainment figures. The logistics of putting together the August 28, 1963, event were an enormous challenge. Organizers had to plan, for example, for inclement weather, medical emergencies, transportation, sanitation, drinking water, and food. They also needed to coordinate speakers and to mobilize members of black communities nationwide who would attend. In

John Lewis, Whitney Young, A. Philip Randolph, Martin Luther King, Jr., James Farmer, and Roy Wilkins meet to discuss the March on Washington.

the meantime, ever worried by the prospect of social disturbances, President Kennedy readied several thousand soldiers for riot control.

The response from Americans staggered the organizers. By the morning of the march, more than a quarter million people had descended on Washington from every state in the Union. They arrived in 21 chartered trains, in caravans of buses and cars, on bicycles, and on foot. One fellow rollerskated to the march from Chicago. Men and women, old and young, black and white, made their way to the summertime shadows of the Washington Monument. Although the occasion was sometimes festive, the mood was serious. Few knew of the behind-the-scenes crisis threatening to destroy the semblance of unity among sometimes rival civil rights groups.

But as folk singers such as Joan Baez, Odetta, Peter, Paul, and Mary, and Bob Dylan entertained the estimated quarter of a million people who assembled, march organizers worked to get SNCC leader John Lewis to temper his speech. Lewis's prepared text bristled with anger. In a shorthand fashion he recalled the painful lessons sandwiched between the Birmingham campaign and the Washington march. In that period bombs had exploded in Birmingham; civil rights workers June Johnson, Annell Ponder, and Fannie Lou Hamer endured a tortuous beating at the hands of Winona, Mississippi, police; Mississippi NAACP leader Medgar Evers was assassinated in his own driveway; and the Highlander Folk School in Tennessee was burned to the ground.

Lewis eventually agreed to the pleadings of Randolph, not because Washington area clergy threatened to boycott the affair, but because he respected and understood the power of the moment. Nonetheless Lewis advised those watching and listening that blacks would not go slow. He told the gathering, "We shall crack the South into a thousand pieces and put them back together in the image of democracy."

Though Lewis offered perhaps the most forceful message of the day, it was Martin Luther King, Jr.'s speech that became a sort of national motto. Fusing classical philosophy to the oral traditions of the black Baptist Church, King preached that day about an America that could be. He shared his dream of a day when race did not matter: "I have a dream that my four little children will one day live in a nation where they will not be judged by the color of their skin but by the content of their character. I have a dream today!"

King's speech—and the entire march—energized the black community with the hope of justice. Then on Sunday, September 15, 1963, little more than two weeks after the March on Washington, a package of dyna-

Interracial marchers make the movement's aims clear: equal job opportunities, integrated schools, and the right to vote.

mite ripped through the Sixteenth Street Baptist Church in Birmingham while worshippers were preparing for church services. When the smoke cleared, four young girls—ages 11 to 14—lay dead. Addie Mae Collins, Denise McNair, Carole Robertson, and Cynthia Wesley had not taken part in earlier demonstrations, but their young faces, appearing in newspapers worldwide, became instant symbols of both the tragedy of racism and the hope of the civil rights struggle. In his eulogy, Martin Luther King, Jr., encouraged his followers not to give up, for "The innocent blood of these little girls may well serve as the redemptive force that will bring new light to this dark city. . . . Indeed, this tragic event may cause the white South to come to terms with its conscience."

Two months later, violence of another kind erupted in Dallas, and the victim this time was President Kennedy, who had gone to Texas to shore up his Southern base in the Democratic party. The 1964 election was a year away, and signs indicated that the Republicans might nominate the very conservative Barry Goldwater, a senator from Arizona. As his motorcade traveled the streets of Dallas on November 22, the sound of rifle fire rang out. The open limousine carrying Kennedy made him a ready target.

With Kennedy's death, Lyndon Baines Johnson, a Texan and former majority leader in the Senate, was sworn in as the country's new President. Among his first acts was to call for passage of the Civil Rights Act proposed by Kennedy. He told a joint session of Congress, "No memorial or eulogy could more eloquently honor President Kennedy's memory than the earliest possible passage of the civil rights bill for which he fought." Johnson and civil rights activists, among many, viewed the impending bill as the most important civil rights legislation since the end of the Civil War.

As Congress debated the merits of the legislation, blacks in Mississippi were continuing to demand their voting rights. In the fall of 1963, activists launched a Freedom Vote campaign to register voters statewide and to demonstrate the importance of black electoral participation. With help from 60 white students drawn from Northern colleges, canvassers went door-to-door, enduring beatings, intimidation, and the fear of physical injury, to get black Mississippians to vote in a mock election. Nearly 100,000 voted for a Freedom Party slate, thereby indicating what they could do if they had the right to vote.

Following this campaign, longtime SNCC worker Bob Moses proposed an expansion of the earlier effort. He and others had in mind a Freedom Summer, during which white college students, in alliance with local black leadership and blacks active in SNCC, would canvass Mississippi, registering voters and teaching in Freedom Schools. Moses had in mind something other than another mock vote; this time he would register blacks for the coming Presidential election in November 1964. Freedom Summer lasted three months—June, July, and August. About 1,000 volunteers participated, three-quarters of whom were white and 300 of whom were women. The students hailed from Western and Northern colleges and universities. After spending a week in a training session directed by SNCC executive director James Forman in Oxford, Ohio, the first 200 volunteers embarked for Mississippi and the 43 project sites scattered across the state.

Tragically, within the first two days of Freedom Summer, law enforcement officials in Philadelphia, Mississippi, added three new names to the list of martyrs who made the supreme sacrifice on behalf of civil rights. Andrew Goodman was a college student at Queens College in New York and a Freedom Summer volunteer. Michael Schwerner had recently opened the CORE office in Meridian with his wife, Rita. CORE worker James Chaney was the only one who was black and a native Mississipian.

On June 21, 1964, the three had set out for Lawndale to investigate another church burning. Near Philadelphia they were arrested for speeding, but the police let them go. That was the last time anyone other than their murderers saw them alive. Word of their disappearance came quickly. Philadelphia sheriff Lawrence Rainey quipped, "If they're missing, they're

The mothers of James Chaney, Andrew Goodman, and Michael Schwerner at the funeral for Goodman in New York City. The three young civil rights activists were murdered in Mississippi by law officers who were Klansmen.

just hid somewhere trying to get a lot of publicity out of it, I figure." But soon the spotlight on the disappearance of Chaney, Goodman, and Schwerner showed in remarkable detail the horrors of life in Mississippi. One hundred fifty FBI agents, aided by sailors, searched woods and rivers. Investigators did not locate the three men until August 4, after they received a tip from an informant motivated by a $30,000 reward. The three decomposed bodies were found buried under a manmade dam. Later testimony revealed that the bulldozer operator at the dam had been paid by Klan members to hide the bodies there. Each had been shot by a .38-caliber gun; and clearly Chaney had been severely beaten before being shot. The U.S. Justice Department indicted 19 men, including police officers and Klansmen, for the murders; only 7 were found guilty.

The horrifying events caused a few volunteers to drop out, but not many. Many would later recall that the summer of 1964 was a pivotal time in their lives. Many whites experienced the warm fellowship of local black Southerners, who freely adopted them into their lives and communities. Black and white participants struggled with the perceptions and realities of power. Some SNCC and CORE activists complained, for example, that white volunteers too quickly assumed they were experts and leaders. Each group had to be educated and reeducated about the other's abilities and sensibilities. But the politics of leadership was no small matter. The tension soon grew into calls for black control of civil rights groups.

More than anything, however, Freedom Summer highlighted the potential political empowerment of black Mississippians. And it turned the national spotlight on racial violence and voting injustices in the state, forcing the federal government to respond. As August came to a close, more than 80,000 blacks joined the new Mississippi Freedom Democratic party (MFDP). They would use this new strength to wrest changes from the national Democratic party, forcing the national body to undo, reluctantly, the practice of locking blacks out of the Mississippi party.

President Johnson signed the Voting Rights Act in 1965, outlawing all obstacles to black voting and authorizing federal officials to enforce fair voting practices. Martin Luther King, Jr., is seated in the second row, directly behind Johnson, and Robert Kennedy is in the front row, fifth from left.

CHAPTER 7

THE FIRE THIS TIME
◇ ◇ ◇

By 1964, African Americans had much to be optimistic about. The 1963 March on Washington, combined with protests in Birmingham and Mississippi and the much publicized murders of civil rights activists and innocent black children, forced Congress to pass the Civil Rights Act of 1964, which President Lyndon B. Johnson signed into law on July 2. It not only outlawed segregation in public accommodations of every kind throughout the country, but it laid the foundation for federal affirmative action policy. Affirmative action programs were meant to insure that victims of past discrimination would have greater opportunities to find jobs, earn promotions, and gain admission to colleges and universities. In particular, Title VII of the Civil Rights Act outlawed employment discrimination by creating the Equal Employment Opportunity Commission (EEOC) to enforce the law. It not only applied to both governmental and nongovernmental employers but covered labor unions and employment agencies as well. Workers who believed they were discriminated against in the workplace because of their race, sex, creed, color, or religion could file a complaint with the federal government.

But the new law did not dismantle the obstacles to voting that blacks in the South still faced. In the summer of 1964, the Mississippi Freedom Democratic party (MFDP) filed a lawsuit against the Democratic party for discrimination and used the television cameras to take their story to the nation. Fannie Lou Hamer told the world how she had been beaten and tortured by white supremacists simply because "we want to register," and she pointed out that the white Democrats were not even loyal to President Lyndon B. Johnson. Those Democrats vehemently attacked Johnson's candidacy because of his commitment to civil rights and equal opportunity for all. Yet, while Johnson agreed with the MFDP's assessment, he and his party would not recognize its delegates as the legitimate representatives of the state of Mississippi at the Democratic National Convention.

Questioning both the horrors at home and the Democratic party's refusal to take their delegation seriously, Hamer asked, "Is this America? The land of the free and the home of the brave?" Johnson's response was to strike a deal: he signaled that he was prepared to select the liberal Minnesota senator Hubert H. Humphrey as his running mate, if MFDP delegates and their surrogates cooperated by allowing the delegation to remain intact, with one modification. Two members of the MFDP would sit as members of the Mississippi delegation, while other MFDP delegates would attend the convention as observers. Although Martin Luther King, Roy Wilkins, executive secretary of the NAACP, and several mainstream black leaders urged the MFDP to accept the compromise, they refused. Most MFDP delegates felt the compromise minimized their claim of truly representing Democrats in Mississippi. Responding to criticism for walking away from the 1964 convention with "nothing," Unita Blackwell explained: "You know, we is going back with something. We're going back with our dignity."

When election day arrived, all of Mississippi's electoral votes went to archconservative Republican Barry Goldwater. Indeed, the Republican

President Johnson consulted with black leaders as he planned a massive War on Poverty. Here, Roy Wilkins of the NAACP, James Farmer of CORE, Martin Luther King, Jr., and Whitney Young of the National Urban League meet with the President in 1964.

party made history, not only winning the state of Mississippi for the first time but also declaring victories in Alabama, Georgia, South Carolina, and Louisiana. The Democratic party's failure to fully embrace Mississippi's black voters signaled the beginning of the end of the solid Democratic South.

Johnson won by a landslide, but the failure of the capital-D Democratic party to support small-d democratic forces in the South and the willingness of Martin Luther King and other national civil rights figures to go along with Johnson struck a blow to the movement. Increasingly, local activists in the rural South, SNCC activists, and urban activists associated compromise with weakness.

Less than a year later King supported another compromise that would further damage and divide the movement. It involved a struggle in Selma, Alabama, where SNCC activists had been locked in a battle with local forces and Governor George Wallace, who used brutal violence to suppress the movement there. After SNCC organizer Jimmie Lee Jackson was shot by a state trooper as he tried to shield his mother from officers' billy clubs during a civil rights demonstration, SNCC and SCLC decided to hold a march from Selma to Montgomery on March 7, 1965. After calling for the march, however, King reconsidered after a tortuous conversation with Attorney General Nicholas Katzenbach. It was clear

Thousands of activists followed the funeral procession of Jimmie Lee Jackson, a young local voting rights worker who was killed by police gunfire in Marion, Alabama, in 1965 during the Selma campaign.

that President Johnson did not want the march to happen, because the potential violence would generate bad publicity and, from his perspective, jeopardize his relations with Southern Democrats. Worried that his defiance of Johnson's wishes might undermine the goal of passing a voting rights bill, King decided to cancel the march at the very last minute. He and Ralph Abernathy left town, announcing that they had to minister to their congregations.

But the young people of SNCC were not about to postpone the march. They convinced SCLC leader Hosea Williams to go on with it, with or without King. (Many marchers, however, did not know what had happened and were surprised by King's absence.) But they never made it; the police and state troopers brutally attacked the racially mixed crowd as it reached the Edmund Pettus Bridge, forcing the marchers to turn back. Three days later, amidst criticism for his absence, King decided to lead another group of 3,000 people, who had answered the call to go to Selma and complete the march, across the bridge. But unbeknownst to the crowd he had made a secret agreement with Attorney General Katzenbach to retreat as soon as they came up against the state troopers. So when King and the march leaders got within 50 feet of the troopers' blockade, they kneeled, prayed, and, as they rose, called on the marchers to retreat. Angry and confused, the marchers did what they were told, many SNCC activists singing "Ain't Gonna Let Nobody Turn Me 'Round" as they made their retreat. The march was eventually held a few weeks later, after much negotiation with the Johnson administration and Governor Wallace.

Despite its fits and starts, the Selma march contributed to the passage of an important piece of legislation by the federal government: the Voting Rights Act of 1965. Signed into law on August 6, 1965, the act prohibited states from imposing literacy requirements, poll taxes, and similar obstacles to the registration of black voters. Of course, the 15th Amendment to the Constitution, passed almost a century earlier, was supposed to guarantee this right to vote, but a federal system of "states' rights" had allowed Southern states to deny black people voting privileges through such measures as the poll tax, literacy tests, and grandfather clauses (until 1939).

With the Voting Rights Act, however, blacks could not be denied the vote any more. Federal examiners were now sent South to safeguard black citizens' right to register and vote. The impact of the act was dramatic: between 1964 and 1969, the number of black adults registered to vote

After watching on TV as troopers attacked marchers in Selma, Viola Liuzzo, a white woman from Michigan and one of the few white members of the NAACP, drove down to Alabama to offer her help. While driving along the Selma highway with a black man who was helping her transport marchers, she was spotted by Klansmen who noticed her out-of-town plates. After a high-speed chase, the Klansmen pulled up alongside Liuzzo's car and shot her in the head.

On March 9, 1965, Alabama state troopers blocked the march of civil rights activists at Selma's Edmund Pettus Bridge. An earlier effort was halted when officers beat and teargassed the marchers. The march to Montgomery was finally completed on March 25.

increased from 19.3 percent to 61.3 percent in Alabama, 27.4 percent to 60.4 percent in Georgia, and 6.7 percent to 66.5 percent in Mississippi. It took several more years before blacks turned the right to vote into electoral might.

The victory was bittersweet. King's role in the Selma march tarnished his reputation in the eyes of his followers. As respect for King's ideas and strategies began to wane among young people, groups such as SNCC began to envision new, more militant strategies. It became clear—from the failure of the MFDP at the 1964 Democratic National Convention to the Selma fiasco—that African Americans could not always rely on the federal government for support. A new generation of activists realized that black people needed more than friends in high places; they needed power.

Within SNCC, a recent Howard University graduate named Stokely Carmichael quickly emerged as a voice of uncompromising militancy and, later, black nationalism. Born in Trinidad and raised in New York City, Carmichael had been associated with interracial radical movements since high school. Like many of his contemporaries, he joined the civil rights movement but never fully embraced the philosophy of nonviolence. He and several other SNCC activists began carrying guns to protect themselves from violence. Carmichael led a militant voter registration campaign, organizing open rallies and marches for black rights in the heart of the Black Belt—with its long history of white violence and terrorism against black sharecroppers. In Lowndes County, Alabama, in 1965, he founded the Lowndes County Freedom Organization (LCFO). An all-black group, (mainly because whites would not join), the LCFO adopted the symbol of the black panther because, according to its chairman, John Hulett, the panther will come out fighting for its life when cornered. "We felt we had been pushed back long enough," Hulett explained, "and that it was time for Negroes to come out and take over."

The LCFO was only the beginning of the new black militancy. A few months later, a group of black SNCC activists in Atlanta circulated a position paper calling on white members to leave the organization and devote their attention to organizing white people in their own communities. Although most SNCC members, black and white, opposed this position, it became clear to many white activists that the character of the movement had changed profoundly. Several leading white figures resigned voluntarily or were forced to leave because, in their view at least, the political climate had become intolerable. Carmichael had successfully contested John Lewis for the chairmanship of SNCC and he, along with other SNCC militants such as veteran organizer Willie Ricks, began questioning the movement's

Stokely Carmichael and demonstrators attempted to march on the Alabama capitol in June 1967. But when police blocked their way, Carmichael motioned for them to sit down in the street rather than retreat.

integrationist agenda. Then, during the summer of 1966, the slogan "Black Power" emerged full-blown within SNCC as well as within the Congress of Racial Equality (CORE).

On June 5, James Meredith, the first black student admitted to the University of Mississippi, initiated a march from Memphis, Tennessee, to Jackson, Mississippi, in order to mobilize black Mississippians to register to vote. A few hours into the march, however, Meredith was shot and the march came to an abrupt end. Martin Luther King, Jr., Carmichael, and CORE leader Floyd McKissick decided to go to Memphis in order to finish the march to Jackson. From the very beginning, however, tensions between King and Carmichael created tensions within the ranks. Carmichael insisted that the Deacons for Defense, an armed black self-defense group based in Louisiana, provide cover for the marchers—a request to which King reluctantly agreed. At the same time, SNCC activist Willie Ricks began to promote the slogan "Black Power" among the membership, who seemed to embrace it enthusiastically. While King called it "an unfortunate choice of words," McKissick embraced it. As he explained, "Black Power is not Black supremacy; it is a united Black voice reflecting racial pride in the tradition of our heterogeneous nation. Black Power does not mean the exclusion of White Americans from the Negro Revolution; it means the inclusion of all men in a common moral and political struggle."

Not everyone agreed with this definition, of course, but it quickly became clear during the summer of 1966 that the issue of "Black Power" would transform the movement in multiple ways. Tired and impatient with the slow pace of the civil rights establishment, a new attitude overtook the movement: no more compromise, no more "deals" with white liberals, no more subordinating the movement to the needs of the Democratic party. Out of bitter disappointment rose this new slogan.

The sources of "Black Power" are as varied as its meanings. Of course, there is nothing new about the idea of "Black Power": Marcus Garvey, founder of the worldwide black nationalist organization called the Universal Negro Improvement Association in 1916, had called for black self-reliance and the creation of autonomous black institutions at least five decades earlier, and before him there had been an array of movements and thinkers expressing similar ideas. And the slogan itself, "Black Power," had been used by writer Richard Wright and New York congressman Adam Clayton Powell well before the 1960s. But like any slogan or set of ideas, the context determines its meaning. The "Black Power" of the 1960s had

The 1966 "March against Fear" in Mississippi was initiated by James Meredith. After Meredith was shot, Martin Luther King, Jr., (front center) and others took over the march. Black militants, however, denounced their tactics of nonviolence and urged blacks to defend themselves against attacks.

roots in the Southern freedom movement itself, in the many compromises made by mainstream leaders, and in the recognition that ending Jim Crow was not enough to win full equality or political power. It also had roots in the increasingly black cities of the North and South, where poverty and police brutality were becoming increasingly visible. And it was nourished by the growing popularity of black nationalism—the idea that black people constitute a single community, if not a "nation," within the United States and therefore have a right to determine their destiny—as expressed by people such as former North Carolina NAACP leader Robert Williams, as well as SNCC leaders such as H. Rap Brown and Stokely Carmichael.

Perhaps *the* most important and controversial progenitor of the Black Power movement was Malcolm X. For many young people, particularly those in the civil rights movement, Malcolm's uncompromising stance toward white supremacy and his plainspoken oratory on black history, culture, and racism deeply affected a new generation of activists. Even efforts to portray Malcolm in a negative light, such as the special 1959 television documentary on the Nation of Islam called "The Hate That Hate Pro-duced" revealed to many black viewers Malcolm's critique of nonviolence and of the strategy to ally with white liberals. He clearly saw the need for a movement in the urban North, one that would focus on the needs of the poor and deal with pressing issues such as police brutality, crumbling schools, and the lack of jobs. While preaching black self-reliance, he also attacked mainstream civil rights leaders for being sellouts. "The black masses," he argued, "are tired of following these hand-picked Negro 'lead-ers' who sound like professional beggars, as they cry year after year for white America to accept us as first-class citizens." Likewise, in his speech before the Northern Negro Grass Roots Leadership Conference in Detroit in 1963, he insisted that the masses had no authentic spokespeople among the "legitimate" black leaders. These men, he said, were "handpicked" by white men in power and thus did not represent the wants and needs of ordinary black people. Self-proclaimed Negro leaders were not just misled; their job was to mislead, to keep black folks in check.

These civil rights leaders, Malcolm said, were leading a nonviolent Negro revolution, when what was needed was a black revolution. Whereas the Negro wants to desegregate, he said, the black demands land, power, and freedom. Whereas the Negro adopts a Christian philosophy of "love

The newspaper of the Nation of Islam, Muhammad Speaks, *helped spread the Black Muslim message.*

thy enemy," the black has no love or respect for the oppressor.

As long as Malcolm remained in the Nation of Islam, he was compelled to conceal his differences with Elijah Muhammad. But as Malcolm became more popular, the tensions between the two men became increasingly evident. The final blow came when Malcolm discovered that the NOI's moral and spiritual leader had fathered children by two former secretaries. The tensions became publicly visible when Muhammad silenced Malcolm for remarking after the assassination of President John F. Kennedy that it was a case of the "chickens coming home to roost." Malcolm's point was that the federal government's inaction toward racist violence in the South had come back to strike the President. When Malcolm learned that Muhammad had planned to have him assassinated, he decided to leave the NOI. On March 8, 1964, he announced his resignation and formed the Muslim Mosque, Inc., an Islamic movement devoted to working in the political sphere and cooperating with civil rights leaders. Despite his criticisms of black leadership, Malcolm had always said that he should be actively involved in the struggles in the South and elsewhere, but Elijah Muhammad's rule that NOI members not participate in politics had hampered Malcolm. Free of the Nation of Islam, Malcolm sought alliances with those willing to work with him.

That same year he made his first pilgrimage to Mecca—the holy city of Islam, in Saudi Arabia. "My pilgrimage broadened my scope," he pointed out in his autobiography. "In two weeks in the Holy Land, I saw what I had never seen in thirty-nine years here in America. I saw all *races*, and all *colors*—blue-eyed blonds to black-skinned Africans—in true brotherhood!" During his trip he changed his name to El-Hajj Malik El-Shabazz and embraced the multiracial Islam he found during his pilgrimage. He publicly acknowledged that whites were no longer devils, though he still remained a black nationalist and staunch believer in black self-determination and self-organization.

During the summer of 1964 Malcolm formed the Organization of

Martin Luther King, Jr., and Malcolm X met accidentally and amicably in Washington in 1964. Despite their differences in style and philosophy, they shared many of the concerns, goals, and risks of freedom movement leadership.

Afro-American Unity (OAAU). Inspired by the Organization of African Unity, made up of the independent African states, the OAAU's program combined advocacy for independent black institutions (for example, schools and cultural centers) with support for black participation in mainstream politics, including electoral campaigns. Following the example of Paul Robeson and W. E. B. Du Bois, who had submitted a petition to the United Nations in 1948 claiming that black people in the United States were victims of genocide, Malcolm planned to submit a similar petition in 1965. The UN petition documented human rights violations and acts of genocide against African Americans. Unfortunately, Malcolm and members of the OAAU never had a chance to submit the petition: on February 21, 1965, he was assassinated by gunmen affiliated with the NOI.

Malcolm had known he was in danger ever since he had left the NOI. He received regular death threats and was constantly followed by suspicious characters. One week before his murder, his home in Queens, New York, was firebombed. He had even begun to carry a gun for protection. But on Sunday, February 21, as he took the stage to speak to a small audience at the Audubon Ballroom in Harlem, two gunmen stood up and opened fire. One got away, but the crowd stopped the other, a Muslim named Talmadge Hayer. (One year later, Hayer was convicted of the murder of Malcolm.) The OAAU died with Malcolm X.

Although Malcolm left no permanent organizations (the Muslim Mosque, Inc., collapsed soon after his death), he did exert a notable impact on the civil rights movement in the last year of his life. Black activists in SNCC and CORE who had heard him speak to organizers in Selma just weeks before his death began to support some of his ideas, especially on armed self-defense, racial pride, and the creation of black-run institutions. Ironically, Malcolm's impact on black politics and culture was greater after his death than before it. In fact, not long thereafter, the Black Power movement and his ideas about community control, African liberation, and race pride became extremely influential. His autobiography, written with Alex Haley—the future author of *Roots,* the fictional account of one African-American family and its heritage—become a movement standard. Malcolm's life story proved to movements such as the Black Panther party, founded in 1966, that ex-criminals and hustlers can be turned into revolutionaries. And arguments in favor of armed self-defense—certainly not a new idea in African-American communities—were renewed by the publication of Malcolm's autobiography and speeches.

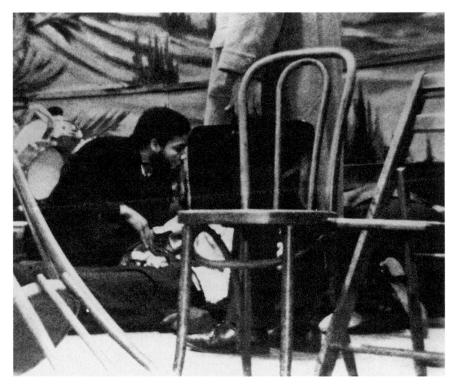

On February 21, 1965, gunshots rang out, and Malcolm X fell onto the stage of the Audubon Ball-room in Harlem, where he was addressing an audience of black activists.

One of the first radical organizations to be inspired by Malcolm's ideas was the Revolutionary Action Movement (RAM). It originated neither in the South nor in the Northeast. Rather, its founders were a group of black Ohio students at Case Western Reserve University in Cleveland, Central State College, and Wilberforce University. Active in SNCC, CORE, and local chapters of Students for a Democratic Society (SDS), a predominantly white national student group that emerged during the Vietnam War protests, this gathering began meeting in 1961 to discuss the significance of Robert Williams's armed self-defense campaign in North Carolina and his subsequent flight to Cuba. Led by Donald Freeman, a student at Case Western Reserve, the group agreed that armed self-defense was a necessary component of the black freedom movement and that activists had to link themselves to anticolonial movements around the world. Freeman was influenced by Malcolm X's speeches and the writings of an independent black Marxist intellectual named Harold Cruse, who argued that African Americans themselves lived under colonialism inside the United States. Freeman hoped to transform the group into a revolutionary movement akin to the Nation of Islam but one that would adopt the direct action tactics of SNCC. By the spring of 1962, they became the Revolutionary Action Movement (RAM).

Although RAM's leaders decided to organize it as an underground movement, it did attract activists across the nation. In the South, RAM built a small but significant following at Fisk University in Nashville, the training ground for many leading SNCC activists. In northern California, RAM grew primarily out of the Afro-American Association, a student group founded in 1962 based at Oakland's Merritt College and the University of California at Berkeley. Never a mass movement, RAM had a radical agenda that anticipated many of the goals of the left wing of the Black Power movement. Its 12-point program called for the development of freedom schools, national black student organizations, rifle clubs, a guerrilla army made up of youth and the unemployed, and black farmer cooperatives— not just for economic development but to keep "community and guerrilla forces going for a while." They also pledged support for national liberation movements in Africa, Asia, and Latin America as well as the adoption of socialism to replace capitalism across the globe. By socialism, they meant a system whereby working people share the fruits of their labor. The land and factories would not be owned by private individuals but by the work- ers. The goal of labor would not be to enrich specific individuals but to improve the quality of life for all.

RAM members were not just radical socialists; they saw themselves as colonial subjects fighting a war for independence. They developed this view by listening to Malcolm X and reading the works of Frantz Fanon, a brilliant young psychiatrist from Martinique who devoted his life to Algeria's battle against French colonialism. Fanon's most famous book, *The Wretched of the Earth* (1963), argued that revolt was necessary not only to overthrow colonialism but to reverse the negative psychological racism that colonial rule has inflicted on subject peoples. They also read the articles of Harold Cruse, who published several essays arguing that African Americans were victims of "internal colonialism." RAM considered black Americans to be colonial subjects who were, in effect, members of the Third World.

After years as an underground organization, a series of "exposés" that ran in *Life* magazine and *Esquire* in 1966 identified RAM as one of the leading extremist groups "Plotting a War on 'Whitey.'" RAM members were not only considered armed and dangerous but "impressively well read in revolutionary literature." Not surprisingly, these highly publicized articles were followed by a series of police raids on the homes of RAM members in

Philadelphia and New York City. In June 1967, RAM members were rounded up and charged with conspiracy to instigate a riot, poison police officers with potassium cyanide, and assassinate NAACP leader Roy Wilkins and National Urban League director Whitney Young. Though the charges did not stick, the FBI's surveillance of RAM intensified. By 1969, RAM had essentially dissolved itself, though its members opted to infiltrate existing black organizations, continue to push the 12-point program, and develop study groups that focused on the "Science of Black Internationalism."

RAM's movement was, in part, based on the assumption that black people had the potential to launch a war against the U.S. government. Writing in exile from Cuba and later China, Robert Williams anticipated black urban uprisings in a spring 1964 edition of *The Crusader*—a publication RAM members regarded as an unofficial organ of their movement. Entitled "USA: The Potential of a Minority Revolution," Williams's article announced, "This year, 1964 is going to be a violent one, the storm will reach hurricane proportions by 1965 and the eye of the hurricane will hover over America by 1966. America is a house on fire—FREEDOM NOW!—or let it burn, let it burn. Praise the Lord and pass the ammunition!!"

Williams was not alone in making this assessment. A year earlier, the writer James Baldwin had predicted that in the coming years race riots would "spread to every metropolitan center in the nation which has a significant Negro population." The next six years proved them right. With riots erupting in the black communities of Rochester, New York City, Jersey City, and Philadelphia, 1964 was indeed a "violent" year. By 1965, these urban revolts had indeed reached "hurricane proportions."

The hurricane also touched the West Coast in the black Los Angeles community of Watts. Sparked when a resident witnessed a black driver being harrassed by white police officers—a frequent occurrence on the streets of Los Angeles—the Watts rebellion turned out to be the worst urban disturbance in nearly 20 years. When the smoke cleared, 34 people had died, and more than $35 million in property had been destroyed or damaged. The remainder of the decade witnessed the spread of this hurricane across America: violence erupted in some 300 cities, including Chicago; Washington, D.C.; Cambridge, Maryland; Providence, Rhode Island; Hartford, Conneticut; San Francisco; and Phoenix. Altogether, the urban uprisings involved close to half a million African Americans, resulted

During the inner-city riots in the summers of 1966 and 1967, looters, arsonists, and vandals took advantage of black unrest.

in millions of dollars in property damage, and left 250 people (mostly African Americans) dead, 10,000 seriously injured, and countless black people homeless. Police and the National Guard turned black neighborhoods into war zones, arresting at least 60,000 people and employing tanks, machine guns, and tear gas to pacify the community. In Detroit in 1967, for instance, 43 people were killed, 2,000 were wounded, and 5,000 watched their homes destroyed by flames that engulfed 14 square miles of the inner city.

Robert Williams was not too far off the mark: a real war erupted in America's inner cities. Elected officials, from the mayor's office to the Oval Office, must have seen these uprisings as a war of sorts because they responded to the crisis with military might at first. Later they turned to a battery of social science investigators, community programs, and short-lived economic development projects to pacify urban blacks. Just as the American military advisers in Southeast Asia could not understand why so many North Vietnamese supported the communists, liberal social scientists wanted to find out why African Americans rioted. Why burn buildings in "their own" communities? What did they want? Were these "disturbances" merely a series of violent orgies led by young hoodlums out for televisions sets and a good time, or were they protest movements? To the surprise of several research teams, those who rioted tended to be better educated and more politically aware than those who did not. One survey of Detroit black residents after the 1967 riot revealed that 86 percent of the respondents identified discrimination and deprivation as the main reasons behind the uprising. Hostility to police brutality was at the top of the list. As one Detroit rioter put it, he was driven to the streets in search for "respect as a man, as a first-class citizen." Likewise, a poll conducted after the Watts rebellion showed that more than half of the African Americans interviewed pointed to economic problems as the cause of the riot. The other explanations included racial humiliation and police repression. Only 8 percent referred to "hoodlums or agitators."

Although Robert Williams, James Baldwin, and many African Americans who survived each day in the crumbling ghettoes of North America knew the storm was on the horizon, government officials and policymakers were unprepared. After all, things seemed to be looking up for black folk: between 1964 and 1969, the median black family income rose from $5,921 to $8,074; the percentage of black families below the poverty line declined from 48.1 percent in 1959 to 27.9 percent in 1969. However, these statistics also reveal a growing chasm between members of a black middle class who were beginning to benefit from integration, affirmative action policies, and a strong economy, and the black poor left behind in deteriorating urban centers. Dilapidated, rat-infested housing, poor and overcrowded schools, the lack of city services, and the disappearance of high-wage jobs in inner-city communities—all contributed to the expansion of urban poverty and deprivation. But there is more to the story: the black freedom movement and the hope it engendered in black communities convinced many blacks that change was inevitable. Some historians have called it "rising expectations"; others simply identified it as "rights consciousness." Either way, an increasing number of African Americans, including the poor, adopted a new attitude for a new day. They demanded respect and basic human rights, expected decent housing and decent jobs as a matter of rights, and understood that social movements and protests were the way to achieve these things. This attitude manifested itself in the daily interactions between blacks and whites. For example, after buses had been desegregated in the South, white residents complained frequently of the growing impudence and discourtesy of black passengers. As one white Birmingham woman complained, "Can't get on the bus and ride to town because the colored have taken the buses."

But the same circumstances that unleashed such fervent opposition to segregation and emboldened ordinary black people to assert their rights also unleashed a more sustained effort on the part of the police to put things back in order. Police repression reached an all-time high between 1963 and the early 1970s—and black male youths from poor communities were involved in the majority of incidents.

There is a similar paradox evident in the growth in the number of welfare recipients during the 1960s. In 1960, 745,000 families received assistance; by 1968 that figure had grown to 1.5 million. The most dramatic increase took place between 1968 and 1972, when the welfare rolls grew to 3 million. On the one hand, the surge in the welfare rolls reflects the expansion of poverty amidst plenty, the growing numbers of poor people (particularly among minority women and children) who needed assistance to survive. But the growth also reflects a "rights consciousness" among welfare recipients inspired by the civil rights and Black Power movements of the period. In 1966, the former associate director of CORE, George Wiley, created the Poverty Rights Action Center (PRAC) in order to help coordinate the activities of numerous local welfare rights organizations that had begun appearing during the early 1960s. Out of discussions within PRAC, Wiley helped found the National Welfare Rights Organization (NRWO) a year later. Led primarily by black female welfare recipients, the NWRO educated the poor about eligibility for assistance under existing laws and pressured welfare agencies to provide benefits without stigmatizing applicants. They demanded adequate day-care facilities and criticized poorly planned job training programs. They attacked degrading, low-wage employment and the practice of scrutinizing women's lives as a precondition for support (such as investigations to determine whether recipients were unwed mothers, had a man living with them, or spent their meager welfare check on things a social worker might find unnecessary, such as makeup). Moreover, they viewed welfare not merely as a gift from the government or a handout but as a right. By emphasizing that welfare was a right, the NWRO stripped welfare of its stigma in the eyes of many poor women and convinced them that they could receive assistance and retain their dignity.

The NWRO was not the only advocate for the increased demands of the black poor. Under President Lyndon Johnson, the federal government launched a "War on Poverty" as part of his overall vision of transforming

America into a "Great Society." Most of the programs that fell under the broad title of the "War on Poverty" were created by the Economic Opportunity Act of 1964. Agencies such as the Job Corps, administered by the Department of Labor, sought to create employment opportunities for the poor. And through the newly created Office of Economic Opportunity (OEO), agencies such as the Legal Services Corporation, to provide civil legal assistance; the Community Action Program; Head Start, a preschool education program; and Volunteers in Service to America (VISTA) sought to provide services for the poor and incorporate them in the decision-making and policymaking process at the local level. The OEO's director, Sargent Shriver, called for the "maximum feasible participation" of the poor in these agencies and, more generally, in the process of solving the problems of poverty.

President Johnson greets a member of the Job Corps, one of many War on Poverty programs. The Job Corps was created to give poor, untrained workers marketable skills. An increasing national concern about pover-ty was one of the important out-growths of the black freedom movement.

The only program that actively tried to implement "maximum feasible participation" was the Community Action Program (CAP). CAP's mission was to coordinate the work of more than a thousand federally funded, neighborhood-based antipoverty agencies and to make new services more accessible to the poor. Unlike other antipoverty agencies, CAP focused its efforts on rehabilitating the entire community rather than poor families or individuals who happened to fall below the pover-ty line. Although CAP quickly earned a reputa-tion for "stirring up the poor," it mainly worked with prosperous local blacks and established black middle-class leadership. Indeed, despite direc-tives from on high calling for maximum feasible participation, urban rebellions from below turned out to be what got the black activists and commu-nity people into the antipoverty agencies.

The bureaucrats and planners who imple-mented these poverty programs conceived of "maximum feasible participation" very differently from groups like the NWRO or leaders of the civil rights movement. After all, they were planned almost entirely by middle-class white men in the Johnson administration who set out to provide "a hand up" to the poorest segment of society—from the ghetto residents in America's sprawling cities, to the Mexican migrants on farms and in barrios in the Southwest, to the poor whites scratching out a living in Appalachia.

Overall, Johnson's Great Society programs did begin to reduce poverty ever so slightly. Ironically, the greatest successes were not products of the Equal Opportunity Act of 1964 but of other programs—notably the expansion of the food stamp program, free school meals and other nutrition projects, and the creation of Medicaid and Medicare programs (which provided the poor and elderly with free health care). But Johnson's War on Poverty fell short of the mark. First, agencies such as the Job Corps focused on job training rather than creating new, decent-paying jobs. Second, Johnson refused to raise taxes in order to pay for these programs, which proved disastrous because he had given the middle class a huge tax cut in 1964 and there was not enough money available. Besides, the cost of fighting the Vietnam War steadily drained federal resources away from the War on Poverty and contributed to rising inflation. Third, the War on Poverty operated from a very limited definition of poverty, one that included only families who fell below a fixed poverty line. The goal was not to change the structure of poverty, to reduce income inequality or help the working poor earn more money; rather, it was to change the behaviors that officials believed led to poverty by providing educational, legal, and job training services to the very poor in order to give them the resources to rise up out of poverty. In other words, the Johnson administration believed the causes of poverty to be culture and behavior rather than political and economic forces. Rather than deal with issues such as low wages, a shortage of well-paying jobs, and blatant racism in employment and labor unions, the proponents of the War on Poverty sought to "correct" poor people's behavior or improve their social skills. The administrators and intellectuals working in these federal programs saw their task in terms of reversing "community pathology," breaking the the "culture of poverty," or restoring the "broken family." The poor, especially the black poor, were considered "disadvantaged."

Most black activists did not believe liberal goodwill, as they viewed it, could eliminate poverty. They viewed the problem in terms of power and unequal distribution of wealth. As NWRO leader George Wiley put it: "I am not at all convinced that comfortable, affluent, middle-class Americans are going to move over and share their wealth and resources with the people who have none. But I do have faith that if the poor people who have the problems can organize, can exert their political muscle, they can have a chance to have their voices and their weight felt in the political process of this country—and there is hope."

Martin Luther King, Jr., concurred. In his book *Where Do We Go From Here?*, King wrote: "The plantation and the ghetto were created by those who had power both to confine those who had no power and to perpetuate their powerlessness. The problem of transforming the ghetto is, therefore, a problem of power." Like Wiley, King had come to the realization that the struggle for racial equality, though hardly over, was not enough. All poor people, he said, irrespective of color, needed to be organized.

So King and the Southern Christian Leadership Conference took the movement to the urban North, settling in Chicago in 1966. They initially tried to build a grass-roots union of poor black residents rather than opening their efforts with a direct-action campaign that would draw media attention, as King and his associates had done in Birmingham three years earlier. When the organizing drive failed to generate much support, King decided to lead a march through a white Chicago neighborhood to demand an end to racial discrimination in housing. King and the SCLC had gone there to appeal to the city, the state, and the nation for open housing for all, and to use the power of love to persuade white racists that segregation was immoral. Instead, King met an angry white crowd raining rocks and bottles on the protesters. In all of his years fighting racism and injustice in the South, he had never seen anything like this before.

The Chicago campaign marked another failure for King. To compound matters, his increasing opposition to the Vietnam War drew fire from nearly every major older mainstream black leader in the country, who feared alienating the volatile President, and further distanced him from the Johnson administration. U.S. involvement in Southeast Asia dated back to the 1950s, when, after the French withdrew from the region, the Eisenhower administration supported a corrupt dictatorship in the southern part of the country, which was already divided by civil war. Under both Presidents Kennedy and Johnson, U.S. intervention escalated; the number of U.S. troops increased from 25,000 in 1965 to 184,000 in 1966. By 1969 more than half a million U.S. personnel were stationed in Vietnam. The official explanation for the war—to roll back communism in Southeast Asia—did not persuade many in the black community. Indeed, some observers regarded the war as a form of genocide because African Americans were overrepresented in combat units and bore a disproportionate share of the casualties. From January to November 1966, for example,

Martin Luther King, Jr., slightly injured by a rock, is led away as angry white home-owners throw rocks at a march for fair housing in one of Chicago's rigidly seg-regated neighbor-hoods in 1966.

black troops made up 22.4 percent of all army casualties while making up about 13 percent of the national population.

Given King's deep and abiding commitment to nonviolence, he was bound to come out openly against the war. And militants in CORE and SNCC had begun issuing antiwar statements as early as 1966. SNCC openly endorsed resistance to the draft. It declared: "Vietnamese are being murdered because the United States is pursuing an aggressive policy in violation of international law." King understood the link between the war abroad and the failure to wage a real war on poverty at home. He pointed out that the United States was spending close to $500,000 to kill each enemy soldier but spent only a paltry $35 a year to help a needy American in poverty. "The promises of the Great Society," he insisted, "have been shot down on the battlefield of Vietnam." The more he criticized the war, the more isolated he became in mainstream civil rights circles. His long-time allies Bayard Rustin, Roy Wilkins, and Whitney Young denounced him publicly, and they were joined by a chorus of distinguished black spokes-men, including Ralph Bunche, Massachusetts senator Edward Brooke, and former baseball star Jackie Robinson. And, of course, this diminished his standing with the White House. But King's national, and international, rep-utation after winning the 1964 Nobel Peace Prize meant he could not be ignored entirely.

As he endured criticism from white and black friends, King became more radical in key respects. He became more committed than ever to organizing the poor and he openly rejected liberal reform as the strategy for change. "For years I labored with the idea of reforming the existing institutions of society, a little change here, a little change there. Now I feel quite differently," he said in 1966. Indeed, he had become a revolutionary. In a statement that combined echoes of the Montgomery bus boycott days with the visions of radicals like Malcolm X and Robert Williams (but with-out the violence), King described the black freedom movement as part of a larger international struggle between the dispossessed and the powerful:

> The storm is rising against the privileged minority of the earth, from which there is no shelter in isolation or armament. The storm will not abate until a

just distribution of the fruits of the earth enables men everywhere to live in dignity and human decency. The American Negro . . . may be the vanguard of a prolonged struggle that may change the shape of the world, as billions of deprived shake and transform the earth in their quest for life, liberty, and justice.

To make this vision a reality, King and his aides at SCLC planned a massive Poor People's Campaign on Washington to take place in the spring of 1968. The march was to bring thousands of poor people from all ethnic and racial backgrounds to demand, among other things, a federally supported guaranteed income policy.

Despite plans for a new campaign, the movement and the criticisms had taken their toll on King. Many friends and associates described him as tired and depressed. He talked openly of death—his own death. As he fretted in the first months of 1968, behind the scenes King and his associates vigorously debated the wisdom of the Poor People's Campaign in Washington. A few encouraged King to support their call for a civil disobedience campaign that would close key streets in the nation's capital. Bayard Rustin, among others, considered such a strategy pure folly, given the outbreaks of violence that had marred the public landscape since 1965. King, moreover, worried that too little had been done to recruit those of all races who were very poor and chronically unemployed.

Meanwhile, in February 1968, in Memphis, another battle erupted, this one between municipal workers who sought union recognition and city officials who refused such recognition. Black garbage collectors in the city fumed when 22 of them were sent home without pay due to bad weather, while white workers were allowed to stay and were paid. The 1,300 members of AFSCME Local 1733, a nearly all-black local representing the sanitation workers, refused to let the issue die; they demanded that the city acknowledge their union and refused to work otherwise. Memphis Mayor Henry Loeb refused to negotiate with the men or anyone else. Residents of the black community joined the men, boycotting downtown merchants and triggering a 35 percent loss of profit. Still the mayor refused to budge. And following an unsuccessful public meeting, a confrontation with police resulted in an ugly moment of violence—onlookers overturned police cars, and the police indiscriminately maced and clubbed everyone in their way.

Seeking to dramatize the plight of black workers and force the city to the bargaining table, longtime civil rights activist and minister of Centenary Methodist Church James Lawson placed a call to King for assistance. The

A mule-drawn farm wagon, symbol of the Poor People's Campaign, bears the casket of Martin Luther King, Jr., through the streets of Atlanta after his funeral. Hundreds of thousands of mourners lined the streets to share their great loss.

fusing of race and economics had by now been a chief concern for King for several years. Still he put Lawson off at first, pleading fatigue and a tight schedule. King did go to Memphis and addressed more than 15,000 on the evening of March 18. He then promised to return the next week, a promise broken only by a rare foot of snow that forced a postponement of the march he was to have joined. In the interim, further negoitations with city officials produced little. On March 28 he did return, prepared to fight until victory was won.

Speaking before a black audience on April 3, King predicted that the Memphis sanitation workers' struggle would succeed. But in midstream, when the audience rose with his inspirational tone, King's speech changed rather abruptly. Sweat pouring down his face, he closed with these famous and fateful words:

> I don't know what will happen now. But it really doesn't matter to me now. Because I've been to the mountaintop. I won't mind. Like anybody, I would like to live a long life. Longevity has its place. But I'm not concerned about that now. I just want to do God's will. And He's allowed me to go up to the mountain. And I've looked over, and I've seen the promised land. . . . I may not get there with you but I want you to know tonight that we as a people will get to the promised land. So I'm happy tonight. I'm not worried about anything. I'm not fearing any man. "Mine eyes have seen the glory of the coming of the Lord."

The following evening, April 4, 1968, King was fatally shot by a white man named James Earl Ray. For some inexplicable reason, the police who had been guarding King's hotel happened to be absent at the time of his assassination. Although they caught the assailant, America lost a visionary.

The response to King's death was immediate and varied. Some white students at the University of Texas at Arlington screamed with glee, joyous that an assassin's bullet had taken out the "troublemaker" King. At the same time the *New York Times* editorialized, "Dr. King's murder is a national disaster." And that it was: major riots engulfed Washington, D.C., Baltimore, and Chicago. All told, more than 100 cities suffered from rioting after the assassination of King, leaving 39 people dead and millions of dollars' worth of property destroyed. President Johnson declared April 7, 1968, a day of mourning, and in tribute to the man whose death brought condolences from leaders and citizens around the world, the country flew its flag at half mast. Between King's death and his funeral on April 9, Coretta Scott King and her children led a silent, peaceful march through the streets of Memphis.

On the hot, humid April day of the funeral, thousands of schoolchildren sat transfixed as black-and-white televisions were hauled into classrooms so that the nation could collectively mourn King's passing. What they witnessed that day was a unique assembly. In the Ebenezer Baptist Church in Atlanta sat Vice President Hubert Humphrey, Presidential aspirants Democrat Robert Kennedy and Republican Richard Nixon, civil rights warriors young and old, Jacqueline Kennedy, who a few years earlier had suffered the loss of her own husband, as well as an assortment of friends, acquaintances, and loved ones. Ralph David Abernathy eulogized his old and dear friend. At Coretta King's insistence, Martin offered his own eulogy, too, as a tape recording of his "A Drum Major for Justice" sermon played for all to hear. That voice, deep and rich, so full of vitality, reminded all of the man who was made by the needs of his time.

A simple cart pulled by two mules hauled King's draped casket to its final resting place. His grave marker told the world what his life had come to symbolize:

FREE AT LAST, FREE AT LAST
THANK GOD ALMIGHTY
I'M FREE AT LAST.

"Today you have a new generation of black people who have come on the scene, who have become disenchanted with the entire system, who have become disillusioned over the system, and who are ready now and willing to do something about it."
—Malcolm X—

CHAPTER 8

WHERE DO WE GO
FROM HERE?
◇ ◇ ◇

O
ne year before his murder in 1968, Martin Luther King, Jr.,
published the book *Where Do We Go From Here: Chaos or
Community*? More than the title itself, the subtitle captured what the year 1968 felt like to many Americans. With
increasing regularity young men were fleeing the nation to
escape the draft or returning from Vietnam in body bags.

Thousands of miles from that war, American support for a declining
Portugal as it struggled to hang on to its African colonies in Mozambique,
Angola, and Guinea-Bissau produced another kind of chaos. For those
African Americans paying attention to liberation campaigns on the African
continent, the support revealed the degree to which the United States
would resort to violence to prop up an aging colonial power. The U.S. government supplied the Portuguese with military advisors and many weapons,
including napalm bombs that were dropped on towns and villages where
African nationalists had established bases.

Back in the United States, 1968 was a year of unprecedented chaos
and considerable violence. Inner-city neighborhoods, such as Washington,
D.C., Chicago, and Memphis, visited by race riots, continued to burn; incidents of police brutality rose steadily; dozens of black activists committed
to protecting their communities from police violence were embroiled in
several shoot-outs with law enforcement officials; and political assassina-
tions continued. Just weeks after the country watched the burial of Martin
Luther King, Jr., a gunman named Sirhan Sirhan fatally shot Democratic
party Presidential candidate Robert F. Kennedy.

Liberals sought to turn this chaos into "community," to stem the
country's division into two nations, one black and the other white. This was
certainly the goal outlined in the report of the National Advisory Com-

*Malcolm X is high-
lighted on this 1969
poster supporting the
militancy of the
Black Power move-
ment. The photo at
top left shows the
riots in Washington,
D.C.; men and
women at the top and
bottom raise their
fists in the Black
Power salute.*

mission on Civil Disorders, a Presidentially appointed committee whose study of the causes of urban uprisings was also published in 1968. Better known as the Kerner Commission (named after Ohio governor Otto Kerner, the commission's head), its report acknowledged the urgent need for the government to bridge the widening gulf between blacks and whites. The report recommended massive job training and employment programs, educational improvements, an overhaul of the welfare system, and a plan for integrating blacks into the nation's mainstream.

The authors of the report, a predominantly white group of liberal social scientists and policy-makers committed to racial integration and ending poverty, made what seemed to many Americans a bold and startling claim: that racism was endemic to U.S. society. Racism was not merely the bad behavior of a few individuals but operated through institutions and forces of power. Thus in order to eliminate racism, massive changes in American institutions needed to take place. As the authors wrote, "The essential fact is that neither existing conditions nor the garrison state [referring to the massive numbers of police and National Guardsmen in riot-plagued communities] offered acceptable alternatives for the future of this country. Only a greatly enlarged commitment to national action—compassionate, massive, and sustained, backed by the will and resources of the most powerful and the richest nation on this earth—can shape a future that is compatible with the historic ideals of American society."

Protesters denouncing the war in Vietnam were one indication of the turbulence in American life in the late 1960s. In the cities, especially, racial tensions often erupted in violence as African Americans fought for equality at home.

While the Kerner Commission proposed a plan to turn "chaos" into "community," African-American activists who embraced the politics of Black Power saw themselves already as community builders. They had previously viewed racism as institutionalized, and most had lost faith in the American creed of justice for all, the goal of integration, or the kindness of white liberals. Instead, they sought to build alternative institutions within black communities, to strengthen the black community itself, and to fight for political and economic power. Of course, precisely what Black Power meant was always open to debate. For some it was a movement for black political power with the hope of making American democracy more open and inclusive for all. For others it meant building black businesses. For many grass-roots activists, Black Power meant creating separate, autonomous institutions within black communities.

The leadership of the Congress of Racial Equality (CORE), a leading force in the civil rights movement, had begun to embrace Black Power around the same time it shifted its focus from large, highly visible direct-action campaigns against segregation to less visible community organizing in poor African-American neighborhoods—especially in the urban North. CORE underwent a change in leadership when Floyd McKissick replaced James Farmer as executive director in January 1966. Farmer, who had been a charter member of the group and took over its leadership in 1961, had been a longtime proponent of integration and direct action, while McKissick had been among the early advocates of Black Power and a strong supporter of Black Power advocate Stokely Carmichael's efforts to build black political strength throughout the South and urban North.

With the shift to a focus on building up black communities, rather than integrating into white ones, CORE's black membership increased dramatically. Some of the increase can be attributed to McKissick. Among his many symbolic and substantive actions, he moved the national office from downtown New York City to Harlem. There, he combined an interest in economic development and an appreciation of cultural training, especially the teaching of African languages. Though he never advocated complete racial separation, CORE's new leader did preach a message of black autonomy and self-determination.

It was Roy Innis, who took over CORE in 1968, who linked black self-determination and black capitalism—that is, getting a fair share of the economic pie, especially control of businesses in urban ghettos. In some ways he saw the black community as a colony within the United States that could become independent only if it had a strong economic base. Innis therefore called for federal funds to establish black businesses. He envisioned a federal system in which black communities would be linked together in a federation, constituting a black "nation within a nation." The U.S. Constitution made no allowances for such a possibility, however. Innis eventually lost faith in black nationalism as a strategy of liberation. By 1972, he had thrown his support behind conservative Republican Richard Nixon and promoted a limited strategy of black enterprise and assimilation.

Others embraced a more conventional—if not conservative—form of economic black nationalism. A small but dominant group came from the rising black middle class. Many college-educated blacks who were nonetheless concerned about affairs within black communities interpreted Black Power to mean black capitalism. In fact, in an age when Black Power evoked fears of bomb-throwing militants and radicals with Afro hairstyles, it is interesting to note that the first Black Power conference was organized by conservative Republican Nathan Wright, and the second was cosponsored by Clairol, a manufacturer of hair care products. Even Republican Richard Nixon, who won the 1968 Presidential election, praised Black Power, since he, like the conservative business daily the *Wall Street Journal,* connected Black Power to black economic self-sufficiency. Expounding on that basic belief, one black journalist wrote in the *Liberator*, a Harlem-based black news magazine: "The primary goal of black people must be economic advancement from which political power and societal equality will result. Therefore, the conservative is the natural ally of the movement for the Black man. Today, as Roy Innis of CORE has attested, only Richard Nixon is . . . hospitable to Black Power."

Nixon was not the only symbol of the white mainstream who embraced black capitalism. A number of corporations, in the spirit of "black power," promoted a black managerial class and supported black capitalism: Xerox sponsored the TV series "Of Black America"; Chrysler put a little money in a black-owned bank; and the lumber and paper products giant Crown Zellerbach set up subsidiaries run by black management. Companies that to date had viewed blacks as no more than consumers even modified their lending policies in the years between 1968 and 1970. Prudential, the large life insurance conglomerate, made more than $85 million in loans to blacks in urban communities, after much of the property it owned and insured in Newark, New Jersey, was destroyed after the 1967 rebellion. Throughout 1968 and 1969, Nixon and other white conservatives supported black economic advancement as an alternative to rebellion or revolution. They believed if people had a real stake in society they would be less inclined to seek its overthrow.

In 1968 and 1969 the federal government and many average citizens openly worried about the overthrow of the government. Many saw chaos and feared true anarchy. College campuses, especially, were sites of social unrest. Antiwar demonstrations, calls for changes in curriculum, attempts to ban the Reserve Officers Training Corps (ROTC, a military training pro-

Roy Innis, who became national director of CORE in 1968, focused his attention on black nationalism. He hoped that black communities could become sufficiently strong and independent to function without support from the white nation.

gram), and other actions caused scores of people, such as California governor Ronald Reagan, to seek the closing of universities. Reagan often threatened to stop the protests at the University of California at Berkeley. He took a step in that direction as early as 1964, when he fired University of California president Clark Kerr for refusing to muzzle students and others attracted to the Free Speech Movement, which was launched on the Berkeley campus in 1964 by those protesting the arrests of students for distributing political literature.

College campuses became a cauldron of black protest, too. In the years 1968–69, 57 percent of all campus protests involved black students. This level reflects both the growing numbers of black students on campuses and the increasing numbers who ended up at predominantly white colleges. Between 1964 and 1970, the number of black college students nearly doubled, from 234,000 to half a million, while the percentage attending black colleges dropped from 51 to 34 percent.

These students were products of the civil rights and Black Power movements as well as the specific circumstances at the colleges themselves. They faced attacks from some white students who were uncomfortable with their increasing numbers on previously nearly all-white campuses; they found the campus environment hostile, given their small numbers, isolation from other students, discrimination by various student groups, and lack of African-American faculty and administrators; and they judged their classes as lacking relevance to their own lives.

Out of this atmosphere emerged the black studies movement. On campuses nationwide, Black Student Unions (BSUs) were formed to advocate further social and curricular changes, especially the introduction of black studies programs. Of course, scholars at many of these institutions and at historically black colleges have taught some aspects of African-American history or studies, but no department committed to developing a broad curriculum based on the lives of African peoples had ever been established. Students took the initiative, first forming political and cultural organizations such as the Afro-American Students Association at Berkeley and Merritt College in Oakland, California, and the Black Student Congress at Columbia University in New York. As early as 1967 students at Howard University called for the creation of a concentrated program in the study of African Americans.

Black students at Cornell University in 1969 launched their own effort to force substantial curricular changes. Since 1967, scores of colleges and universities, both black- and white-dominated, had to address the demands of blacks. In fact, between 1960 and 1969, the scene of the sit-in shifted from the lunch counter to the university president's office. Protests visited campuses as varied as the University of Massachusetts, Duke, Harvard, Columbia, Yale, Simmons College, and Antioch.

At Cornell, a particularly dramatic episode transfixed the nation. Through the mid-1960s Cornell had had a dismal record of attracting and graduating African-American students. But beginning around mid-decade the school began in earnest to recruit blacks. Once there, however, the black students complained of overtly racist acts and general alienation. They also sought to institute a black studies department. After a series of incidents, including the tossing of a burning cross into a dormitory, tensions reached a critical phase, and black students took over part of the student union during Parents Week in April. Fearing more violence, especially given their small numbers (only 250 of the more than 10,000 students on campus were black), a few black students managed to smuggle guns into the union. After long negotiations, which ultimately led to Cornell's first black studies program, the students filed out peacefully and ended the standoff. When the incident ended without loss of life, the country recalled only the image of gun-toting black students. What many outside commentators failed to realize was that students wanted more than freedom by 1969; they wanted liberation, and they were willing to fight for their demands, educational or otherwise.

After enduring racist attacks and harassment by white students, armed black students decided to take over the Cornell University student union in 1969. They negotiated with the administration for the creation of a black studies program, and the incident ended without any fatalities.

The link between liberation and education was not confined to the university. By 1968 the struggle for Black Power in education had reached down to public schools in many locales. More and more community activists began demanding control over local schools. Black parents and teachers objected to a curriculum that excluded Third World cultural perspectives. They objected, too, to the tracking of their children into remedial and special education classrooms, which they considered just another form of segregation; and they objected to the failure to funnel blacks and Latinos into college preparatory classes. More than anything, they objected to the fact that they had so little control over what their children learned.

A bitter 1968 New York City teachers' strike, which pitted largely Jewish schoolteachers against black and Puerto Rican communities in the Ocean Hill–Brownsville section of Brooklyn, came to symbolize the period and its tensions. The inability of New York City to integrate its schools led residents of poor Latino and African-American communities to push for community control. The Board of Education granted approval to Ocean Hill–Brownsville residents to set up a community board with complete authority over the district's elementary schools. The newly formed governing board immediately got into trouble, however, when it attempted to reassign 19 white teachers. District superintendent Rhody McCoy had not taken the usual steps of finding them employment elsewhere, so they were, in effect, fired. Albert Shanker, the president of the United Federation of Teachers (UFT), protested. The union waged six walkouts, or strikes, between May and November 1968, which ultimately led to the termination of the community control program. A compromise, however, did give schools with low overall reading scores some say in who would be hired to teach. Still, members of the UFT were especially angry that community control eroded their ability to protect teachers' jobs—the primary responsibility of the teachers' union. On the other hand, community activists and black teachers affiliated with the African-American Teachers Association (ATA) regarded established white educators and their programs as out of touch with the realities inner-city children had to face. They believed that teachers of their own race were needed to help build self-esteem and create a healthier environment for effective learning.

For some black residents, the fight to transform urban education was merely a small part of a larger revolutionary movement. Organizations sprang up during this period that sought to transform the whole country, to eliminate all forms of inequality and racial discrimination. Perhaps the best-known of the radical black organizations was the Black Panther party (BPP). Although it is often identified as a proponent of Black Power, the BPP was essentially a Marxist organization. Embracing the ideology of the 19th-century German political philosopher Karl Marx, BPP members believed that the poor and oppressed peoples of the world would eventually mount a revolution to overthrow capitalism, an economic system that, Marxists believed, exploited workers.

Calling itself the Black Panther Party for Self-Defense, it was founded in October 1966 in Oakland, California. The group was led by Huey P. Newton and Bobby Seale, former student activists at Merritt College in Oakland. At its founding, the party issued a 10-point program calling for, among other things, full employment, decent housing, relevant education, black exemption from military service, an end to police brutality, freedom for all black prisoners, and trials with juries of their peers. Seeing themselves as part of a global liberation movement, the Panthers also spoke of the black community as a colony inside the United States. Yet, unlike many other black or interracial radical groups of their day, they never advocated secession or the creation of a separate state. Instead, they preferred interracial coalitions when possible. They joined forces with the predominantly white Peace and Freedom party (a third party of socialists and peace activists) and developed strong ties with Students for a Democratic Society (SDS).

In alliance with the Peace and Freedom party, the Black Panther party put up candidates in both the national and California state elections

A 1968 Black Panther rally in New York. Carrying guns and wearing their trademark berets, the Panthers believed blacks should arm themselves against police brutality. Over the next few years, shootouts with police officers and FBI agents were frequent.

Surrounded by body-guards, Huey Newton speaks at a Black Panther convention in Philadelphia in 1970. Earlier, Newton had been jailed on charges of shooting an Oakland police officer, but he was freed after a public outcry against his imprisonment.

of 1968. The coalition's Presidential candidate was Eldridge Cleaver, an ex-prisoner who wrote the best-selling book *Soul on Ice* (1968). He had joined the party in February 1967. As a writer and speaker, Cleaver emerged as the main spokesperson for the Panthers after Bobby Seale was arrested for armed invasion of the State Assembly chamber in Sacramento and Newton was jailed for allegedly shooting an Oakland police officer. The charges against Newton were eventually dropped, but only after a long national campaign to free him.

The Black Panthers felt that armed struggle was the only way to defend the black community from police repression. By carrying loaded firearms in public (which was legal in California at the time), the Panthers drew a great deal of attention from the media and wrath from the police and FBI. Perhaps because of their notoriety, their ranks grew; by 1970 Panther chapters had taken root in 19 states and in more than 30 cities. Equally impressively, chapters appeared in England, Israel, and France.

A deft combination of style and substance accounted for the party's popularity. Early BPP members looked sharp in their all-black outfits of jeans, shirt, beret, and sunglasses. They affected a politics of style, making themselves look daring, mysterious, dangerous, and powerful. But style alone would fail, they quickly realized. As a result, the Panthers sponsored

Testifying before a Senate subcommittee, Police Lieutenant Lawrence Bearse of Jersey City, New Jersey, points to a list of Black Panther demands. These demands, such as "power to control our destinies"—No. 1 on the list—appealed to many African Americans who did not necessarily support the Panthers' methods.

several community-based initiatives in most cities in the country, including clothing drives, a community day-care center, a Panther school, and a free breakfast program. Their free breakfast program provided meals to 200,000 children daily. Most amazingly, they proved that grass-roots movements could make a difference, even when the U.S. government vowed to eliminate the organization by any means necessary.

Federal law enforcement officers, especially the FBI, targeted a growing list of black-run organizations in the late 1960s. Since the mid-1960s the agency had spied on Dr. King, Malcolm X, and other notable black leaders. By 1968 spying had come to include an active policy of group infiltration, in which FBI informants posed as members of radical or militant organizations. Local and federal police began a crackdown. In 1969, for example, police arrested 348 Panthers for a range of offenses, among them murder, rape, robbery, and assault.

The FBI and local police declared war on the Panthers. In 1968 alone, at least eight Black Panthers were killed by police in Los Angeles, Oakland, and Seattle. And the during the following year, two Chicago Panther leaders, Mark Clark and Fred Hampton, were killed in their sleep during an early morning police raid. The violence and constant surveillance by the FBI reflected the position of FBI director J. Edgar Hoover: the only good Panther was a dead Panther. Without question, the FBI helped destroy the Black Panther party.

Yet it was much more difficult to snuff out all who were swayed by the appeal of Black Power. In Detroit, for example, radical Black Power ideology influenced one of the most militant labor movements in the country. Eventually calling themselves the League of Revolutionary Black Workers (LRBW), the group was founded by several young black auto workers, many of whom worked at Detroit's Dodge Main Plant. Led by activists such as Luke Tripp, General Baker, John Watson, Mike Hamlin, and Ken Cockrel, they were a unique bunch. All had been students at Wayne State University and had worked together in a black nationalist organization called Uhuru (Swahili for "Freedom"). Uhuru had been loosely associated with RAM—the same organization from which several founding members of the Black Panther party came.

Two events spurred the creation of the league. The first was the Detroit riots of 1967, which revealed the degree of unrest, poverty, and police brutality in the "Motor City." The Detroit chapter of the NAACP was flooded with complaints about police treatment of African Americans. Even black police officers were subjected to brutality.

The second event was more immediate: on May 2, 1968, General Baker and several other black militants in the Dodge Main Plant led a walkout of 4,000 workers, the first in that factory in 14 years and the first organized and led entirely by black workers. The strike was over a speedup of the assembly line, which in the previous week had increased from 49 to 58 cars per hour. Out of this strike emerged the Dodge Revolutionary Union Movement (DRUM). It was the first of several Revolutionary Union Movements (RUMs) that popped up at auto plants in and around Detroit, and which subsequently led to the formation of the League of Revolutionary Black Workers.

DRUM's specific demands—safer workplaces, lower production demands, an end to racist hiring practices—echoed past grievances. Of course they wanted to win better working conditions and wages for black workers, but their ultimate goal was freedom for all workers—and that meant, in their view, the end of capitalism. DRUM members knew that racism limited the ability of workers to unite, and that white workers, as well as black workers, were hurt by this. But they also argued that white workers benefited from racism in the form of higher wages, cleaner and safer jobs, and greater union representation.

Not everyone in the league agreed as to the best way to achieve Black Power and workers' power. One group, led by General Baker, believed the movement should focus on shop-floor struggles, while Watson, Hamlin, and Cockrel felt that the league needed to organize black communities beyond the factories. Thus, the latter got together and organized the Black Economic Development Conference (BEDC) in the spring of 1969. At the urging of former SNCC leader James Forman, who had recently arrived in Detroit, the league became heavily involved in the planning and running of the conference.

Out of BEDC came Forman's proposal for a Black Manifesto, which demanded, among other things, $500,000,000 in reparations from white churches and synagogues to be used to purchase land in the South, fund black publishing companies, a research skills center, a black Southern university, and a national black labor strike fund. The work in BEDC took the league leadership, of which Forman was now a part, away from its local emphasis. Their efforts led to the founding of the Black Workers Congress (BWC) in 1970. The BWC called for workers' control over the economy and the state to be brought about through cooperatives, neighborhood centers, student organizations, and ultimately a revolutionary party. And they demanded better wages and working conditions for all workers.

Meanwhile, the league's local base began to disintegrate. Dodge had fired several league activists, including General Baker. The General Policy Statement of the league, which based everything on the need for vibrant DRUM-type organizations, seemed to have fallen by the wayside. Divisions between the leadership groups were so entrenched that no one could cooperate any more.

Influenced by events on the factory floor and in the universities, writers laid claim to their own interpretations of Black Power. Starting with John Oliver Killen's 1954 novel *Youngblood,* and increasing in frequency by the mid-1960s, black writers debated whether there was something distinctive about black culture, something that made it different from "white" or European-American culture. The debate had less to do with whether black writers would write about black life—they had been doing so since the days of the first slave narratives in the United States—and more to do with a universal definition of a black aesthetic. By aesthetic, these critics and artists meant elements of style or form that are common in black culture. In the midst of the debates and disagreements that ensued, some sense of a general consensus did emerge. Black was not only powerful—it was beautiful. And it was up to black people to express and celebrate both the power and the beauty.

A 1968 edition of the New Pittsburgh Courier ran this illustration, reflecting the new awareness of African Americans that they had not only black power but black beauty as well.

Thus, the political revolution in black America was accompanied by a profound cultural revolution. A new generation of artists created literature, art, and music that celebrated black people and promoted rebellion against racism and poverty throughout the world. They encouraged African Americans to celebrate their African heritage and to embrace their blackness not as a mark of shame but a symbol of beauty.

To understand this revolution, however, we need to go back to the 1950s, when Africans declared war on European colonialism and began to win their independence. Inspired by Africa's example, jazz pianist Randy Weston recorded the album *Uhuru Afrika* (1960); drummer Max Roach brought together African and African-American musicians to produce *We Insist: Freedom Now Suite* (1960); and the brilliant saxophonist John Coltrane recorded songs such as "Dahomey Dance" (1961), "Africa" (1961), and "Liberia" (1964). African Americans even began to emulate African styles or create new styles that, in their mind, represented African culture. During the early 1960s a number of black women artists—most notably the folk singer Odetta, the jazz vocalist Abby Lincoln, and the exiled South African singer Miriam Makeba—styled their hair in medium to short Afros. They refused to straighten their hair and instead allowed it to grow naturally.

All of these independent cultural developments emerging out of the late 1950s and early 1960s began to coalesce into a full-blown movement just when America's cities began to explode. In 1965, following the assassination of Malcolm X, the poet and playwright Leroi Jones and several other black writers, namely Larry Neal, Clarence Reed, and Askia Muhammad Toure, founded the Black Arts Repertory Theater School (BART) in an old brownstone building on 130th Street in Harlem, New York. With meager support from federal War on Poverty programs, they held classes for Harlem residents and launched a summer arts and culture program that brought music, drama, and the visual arts to the community virtually every day of the week.

Like many artists of his generation, Leroi Jones could not ignore the black freedom movement in his midst. Before founding BART, he was the senior member of the downtown New York literary scene. Born to a working-class family in Newark, New Jersey, Jones attended Howard University (a historically black college), served briefly in the air force, and ended up a struggling writer in New York's Greenwich Village. After the success of his first book of poetry, *Preface to a Twenty Volume Suicide Note* (1961), his first book of prose, *Blues People: Negro Music in White America* (1963), and his first play, *Dutchman* (1964), he no longer had to struggle. Indeed *Dutchman*, a surreal encounter between an educated black man and a white woman who, as a symbolic representative of the racist state, taunts the man and eventually kills him, earned him many awards and accolades. After *Dutchman,* Jones could have pursued a lucrative career as a writer but chose instead to use his artistic insights to build a political movement.

In 1966, a year after founding BART, Jones moved back to his hometown of Newark, started a similar institution called Spirit House, and changed his name to Imamu Amiri Baraka. Although Spirit House also sponsored community arts programs, it developed a more explicit political orientation after Newark's ghettos exploded in 1967. In the aftermath of the riots, Spirit House held a black power conference that attracted several national black leaders, including Stokely Carmichael, H. Rap Brown, Huey P. Newton of the Black Panther party, and Imari Obadele of the newly formed Republic of New Africa (a black nationalist organization that demanded land on which African Americans could settle and form an independent nation, and was partly an outgrowth of RAM). Shortly thereafter, Spirit House became the base for the Committee for a Unified Newark (CFUN) In addition to attracting black nationalists, Black Muslims, and even a few Marxists, CFUN bore the mark of Ron Karenga's US Organization.

Karenga, originally a West Coast leader of RAM, insisted that the crisis facing black America was first and foremost a cultural crisis. He envisioned "US" as a movement of cultural reconstruction, creating a new synthesis between traditional African culture and African-American culture. Drawing on African religions, philosophies, and ideas about family and kin relations, US attempted to create a political movement rooted in communal ties between people of African descent rather than competition or individualism. Although tensions arose between Karenga and some of the Newark activists over his treatment of women and the overly centralized leadership structure CFUN had imported from the US Organization, the movement continued to grow.

In this setting, the search for artistic expression became known as the Black Arts Movement. In addition to Baraka, other leading lights included

James Brown and other artists experimented with music as a way to carry a political message to a mass audience. Soul, especially, was rooted in the black experience—the struggle for power and for a voice.

poets Nikki Giovanni, Don L. Lee (Haki Madhubuti), Jayne Cortez, and Sonia Sanchez; playwrights Ed Bullins, Ben Caldwell, and Jimmy Garrett, to name a few. Although openly critical of whites and brutally critical of blacks who seemed to go along with a system of white supremacy, the members of the Black Arts Movement were important for the innovations they introduced in literary form. Determined to bring poetry and prose to the people, they experimented with freer forms and drew heavily on jazz rhythms and the everyday vernacular language of black folk. They often turned the hip, cool phrases of black youth into hot, angry declarations of war against American racism and exploitation.

While literary artists made an appeal for the hearts and souls of the black majority, it was musicians who achieved mass appeal in the late 1960s, a time of intense experimentation and political expression. Some of them, such as James Brown (known as the "godfather of soul") and poet/singer Gil Scott-Heron, adopted a Black Power stance more clearly than others. Still, the late 1960s were a time of intense experimentation and political expression. Within jazz circles, artists such as saxophonists Ornette Coleman, John Coltrane, Albert Ayler, and Archie Shepp, pianists Cecil Taylor and Sun Ra, and many others, lauded a new sound, variously known as "free jazz," "the new thing," the "jazz avant-garde," or the "new black music." Detractors, on the other hand, called the music "anti-jazz" or "nihilism." Essentially, the new jazz musicians began playing free form, breaking out of traditional harmonies, rhythms, and song structures. Inspired by music from Africa and Asia, they often improvised freely over a single musical phrase. Furthermore, many of these musicians identified with the black arts movement; Ayler, Shepp, Sun Ra, and others performed frequently at BART, and the jazz avant-garde even had its own publications calling for the creation of revolutionary music. The key journal at the time was called the *Gracle: Improvised Music in Transition.* In the *Gracle*, black musicians debated the music's relationship to the movement, thought about ways to fuse music and literature, and discussed the importance of political education for black artists.

Although the jazz avant-garde sought to establish direct ties to black communities, its music never achieved the popularity of "soul" music. The creators of soul (the shorthand for soul music) consciously searched for black roots; their products reflected gospel's major influence. Aretha Franklin's early music, for example, was characterized by gospel-style piano playing.

A product of mid- to late 1960s transformations, soul was also much more political than rock and roll. Its themes have to do with more than equality; they deal with conditions in the urban North such as poverty, the powerlessness of black folk, and drug use. The titles tell the story: James Carr's "Freedom Train," the Chi-Lites' "Give More Power to the People," Tony Clarke's "Ghetto Man," and James Brown's "Say it Loud, I'm Black and I'm Proud."

Still, there was no single ideology of Black Power in soul music. Singers Curtis Mayfield and James Brown simultaneously promoted reform of the system and acceptance into it. The possibility of radical change seems ever present in Mayfield's lyrics, but only as a last resort. Songs like "Move on Up" and "Keep on Keeping On" tell people to keep working hard and fighting and they'll get a share in democracy. Yet "People Get Ready" and "Underground" evoke an image of violent revolution in which a totally new society would emerge from under the ashes of self-destruction. He predicts, or at least hopes, there will be equality in the underground: "We'll all turn black. . . . Color, creed, and breed must go."

James Brown's music as well as his politcal statements were even more contradictory. While recording songs promoting black pride like "Say it Loud, I'm Black and I'm Proud," and "Soul Brother No. 1," he also came out with the patriotic assimilationist tune "America is My Home." After King was assassinated and riots began erupting, Brown went on national television to urge blacks to go back home. He even came out in support of the conservative and sometimes openly racist President Richard Nixon, mainly because of Nixon's advocacy of black capitalism as a way of achieving racial equality.

The Temptations and Marvin Gaye were also politically conscious, but unlike Mayfield, whose songs were of hope and possibility, theirs were songs of pessimism: Gaye's "Inner City Blues," "What's Goin' On?" and the Temptations' "Message from a Black Man," "Cloud Nine," and "Ball of Confusion." In the last, before the chorus, "Ball of Confusion, that's what the world is today," we hear a baritone voice singing "And the band plays on," signaling business-as-usual politics, indifference, and apathy. The "band" is symbolically drowning out the noise of poverty and resistance. The irony of this world as described by the Temptations is captured in the line "The only safe place to live is on an Indian reservation."

As millions of black Americans tuned in to the sounds of soul and jazz, they also tuned in to the dramatic television broadcast from the 1968

Tommie Smith and John Carlos give the Black Power salute at the 1968 Olympic Games as they are awarded the gold and bronze medals in the 200-meter race. Because this action was considered too "political," they were suspended from the Games and stripped of their medals.

Mexico City Olympics. What happened there represented the most international expression of Black Power. To call attention to racism in sports here and abroad, former San Jose State basketball and track and field star Harry Edwards formed the Olympic Project for Human Rights. Its intent was to organize an international boycott of the 1968 games.

Edwards hoped to draw attention both to the treatment of black athletes as well as to the general condition of black people throughout the world. As he put it, "What value is it to a black man to win a medal if he returns to the hell of Harlem?" Specifically, he and others sought to ban athletes from South Africa and Southern Rhodesia (both at the time were white-dominated African countries that segregated and exploited the African population) from the Olympics, the appointment of a black member to the U.S. Olympic Committee, appointment of an additional black coach on the U.S. team, the desegregation of the New York Athletic Club, and the removal of the International Olympic Committee's president, Avery Brundage. Among other things, Brundage was quoted as saying he would sell his exclusive Santa Barbara, California, country club membership before admitting "niggers and kikes" as members.

Instead of boycotting the Olympics, however, black athletes decided to use the event as a way to draw attention to racism and the black struggle. They agreed to wear black armbands and developed strategies to protest during the victory ceremonies. The most famous demonstration involved track stars Tommie Smith and John Carlos, who mounted the awards platform wearing knee-length black socks, no shoes, and a black glove on one hand (Smith also wore a black scarf around his neck). When the band played the U.S. national anthem, they bowed their heads and raised their gloved fists toward the sky in the Black Power salute. In an interview with sportscaster Howard Cosell, the pair explained that the closed-fisted salute symbolized black power and unity; the socks with no shoes represented the poverty most black people must endure; and Smith's scarf symbolized black pride. They bowed their heads in memory of fallen warriors in the black liberation movement, notably Malcolm X and Martin Luther King, Jr.

Although their actions did not harm anyone or incite violence, the U.S. Olympic Committee decided to suspend Smith and Carlos from the games and strip them of their medals for being overtly political. Angered by the decision, many of their fellow black athletes continued to protest. The three U.S. medalists who swept the 400-meter dash wore black berets on the victory stand, as did the 1,600-meter relay team (which also broke the world record). Bob Beamon and Ralph Boston, medal winners in the long jump, wore black socks without shoes to protest both the condition of black people and the treatment of their teammates. And Wyomia Tyus, anchor in the women's 400-meter relay team, dedicated her gold medal to Carlos and Smith.

The political stance of black athletes in Mexico City combined with other examples of forceful advocacy of Black Power to provoke fear and a backlash. By 1969, after passage of the Civil Rights Act of 1964, the Voting Rights Act of 1965, and the Fair Housing Act of 1968, many white Americans began to ask: What more does the Negro want? Dissatisfied with the responses they heard to that question, more and more whites found their own answers in the politics of rage endorsed first by George Wallace and then by Richard Nixon.

George Wallace had surfaced as a national political force in the early 1960s, after he made a highly publicized effort to block the desegregation of the University of Alabama. He had been active in Alabama politics since before the start of World War II. Steeped in the traditions of Alabama and the South, he held views on race that were neither enlightened nor particu-

Standing in front of a banner that actually reads "Courage," George Wallace campaigns in Texas for the 1968 Presidential election. Representing a white backlash to the civil rights agenda, Wallace pledged to end "special privileges" for African Americans.

larly regressive. Each race had its own genius and place in the life of country, he asserted at the time. To him this was less a disputable fact than merely an obvious truth.

He held fast to that view through the Alabama gubernatorial campaign of his mentor "Big Jim" Folsom in the mid-1950s. With the *Brown* v. *Board of Education* decision fresh in people's minds, with Montgomery roiling from the effects of the bus boycott and news of similar boycotts forming across the region, Wallace staked out a new political image. It was an image that distanced him from his mentor, assured his own selection as

178

governor of Alabama in 1962, and forever solidified his reputation as the embodiment of Southern obstruction of black rights.

But it was Wallace the Presidential candidate rather than Wallace the governor who attracted more attention. George Wallace's ascendancy as a legitimate third-party candidate in 1968 signaled a clear backlash. He openly courted whites who felt disenfranchised by governmental policy. For his efforts he won five Southern states in 1968 and between 8 and 15 percent of the vote in more than a dozen Northern and Western states. Before an assassin's bullet nearly killed him in 1972, Wallace had received nearly as many popular votes in the Democratic Presidential primaries as George McGovern, the Democratic party's eventual candidate. Wallace's most important influence, however, may have been inspiring the Republican party to adopt a strategy that catered to white fears of social equality for blacks.

Richard Nixon quickly moved into the political space Wallace had created. Aided by the conservative push in his own party, the electoral appeal of law and order themes in 1968, and his own realization that Republicans could use race as an issue to drive Southern whites into their party, he outlined a plan for what became the Republican party's Southern strategy. Nixon survived his own defeat at the hands of John F. Kennedy in the 1960 Presidential election; he suffered another bitter defeat in the California governor's race in 1962, only to emerge as the Republican standard bearer in 1968. In the interim he crisscrossed the country speaking for other candidates. During this period, he built a strong network among party loyalists.

Moreover, Nixon listened to George Wallace and had come to realize that the former governor of Alabama was not only a formidable adversary but had tapped a sea of resentment in many white communities. Angry whites, upset with advances for blacks, opposed school busing and Supreme Court decisions outlawing school prayer and extending civil liberties. Nixon believed he could effectively tap that resentment. And heading into the spring of 1968, polls showed Nixon tying either Robert F. Kennedy or Hubert H. Humphrey, the two leading contenders for the Democratic nomination. Kennedy's assassination left Humphrey, the old liberal now too closely aligned with Lyndon Johnson's failed social and military policies. Nixon won the election in part due to his ability to channel a racial backlash. This backlash came just as black Americans intensified their demands for social, economic, and political action.

Despite backlash politics and the rising tide of racism, this was also the moment Black Power in some ways entered the realm of electoral politics. Nearly a generation after a new wave of black migrants moved into urban areas, during what became known as the Second Great Migration, their numbers had grown sufficiently—and whites had fled city centers in large enough numbers—to give blacks electoral majorities, or at the very least working margins. This change in the racial makeup of cities improved the likelihood that African Americans could gain a stronger political foothold in major urban centers. In some cases, they were successful. The mayoral victories of Carl Stokes in Cleveland and Richard Hatcher in Gary, Indiana, in 1967 raised black hopes that electoral politics might offer real opportunities, at least at the municipal level. However, despite a growing black electorate in the nation's cities, African Americans held few really important political offices.

Carl Stokes was elected mayor of Cleveland in 1967. As the black urban population increased, so did the hope that African Americans would finally be able to exercise real political power.

During the early 1970s, for example, black elected officials tended to hold low-level city and county jobs, especially in law enforcement, on school boards, and on some city councils. Most of these black elected officials were in the South. The lack of more significant black political representation in big Northern cities where African Americans made up 40 to 50 percent of the population was particularly striking. To pave the way for participation at higher levels of city government, black political leaders worked hard on devising strategies to win local elections.

By the middle of the 1970s, many blacks living in the major cities publicly wondered about what they had inherited. Scarred by racial violence, often abandoned by taxpaying consumers and large corporate and financial interests, many cities, for a time at least, became difficult places to live. Prior to King's murder, scores of black people still held out hope that they could transform America. The Poor People's Campaign in Washington, planned for the spring of 1968, was to have focused the nation's attention on the uneven distribution of wealth. The march occurred, but it failed to incite the federal government to take action.

At the same time, the public mood shifted to a call for law and order instead of a focus on justice for the poor and oppressed. Lyndon Johnson certainly supported the broad outline of the Kerner Commission Report, which called for integrating blacks into the nation's mainstream, but during the last two years of his Presidency, the federal government, from the perspective of many blacks, shifted from reluctant protector to truly hostile adversary. Given free rein by Presidents Johnson and Nixon, J. Edgar Hoover instructed his FBI men to eliminate the vanguard, or liberal and radical leaders, of the freedom struggle. He believed that this would eliminate, or at least neutralize, any form of opposition to government policies.

It would be a mistake, however, to conclude that African Americans had lost the resolve to change things. From voting to dress to music, they still advocated change. The Afro hairstyle, nicely coifed, became a powerful symbol of a new mood and style in the black community. It signified a pride in self and a comfort with what was natural. In music as well, the commitment to change remained ever present, as young black people searched for a sound that expressed new circumstances. Soon, the soul music of the 1960s was overshadowed by funk and disco in the 1970s and by rap in the 1990s.

When the clock ticked off the last minute of 1969 and African Americans took stock of the last few years, they thought not only about the changes they had witnessed but also about the ones they still hoped to see. They knew they were the caretakers of King's dream of living in a nation where character was more important than color. And they knew they had to take charge of their community. After all, the civil rights and Black Power eras had forged change through community action. Although many blacks may have sensed that all progress was tempered by the social, economic, and political realities of a government and a white public often resistant to change, they could not ignore the power of their own past actions. America in 1969 was not the America of 1960 or 1965. At the end of the decade, a chorus could be heard rising from the black community proclaiming, "We changed the world."

EPILOGUE

◇ ◇ ◇

A lthough the freedom movement was based on a clear recognition of the failure of American democracy to address the life of black people, it never confined itself to protesting that failure. Rather, at their best, the freedom workers always insisted on pressing our nation to realize its potential for all people. The men, women, and children who marched, dreamed, organized, sang, and stood firm against the forces of white supremacy were working for us all. They were helping our nation to move away from a condition in which there was much talk about freedom, justice, and democracy for all but also a harsh refusal to apply these great truths to black people. The freedom movement insisted on creating a healthy nation, a nation that "could live at peace with itself," as Martin Luther King, Jr., often put it.

African Americans actually remade postwar America, bringing its racial contradictions to the fore, battering down the barriers of legal segregation, expanding the arena of democracy in campaigns and confrontations that eventually provided inspiration to pro-democracy movements across the globe. At the same time, black people were conquering their old fears, creating new possibilities for themselves and their children, developing freedom-based music and art forms that are now recognized as central parts of American popular culture. Within a few decades, the insistent thrust of the African-American freedom and black identity movements transformed a people, a region, and a nation, and sent new signals of hope around the world.

Through the powerful energies and vision of the black freedom struggle, the way was opened for a new America, one in which all of its people could play a role. After the days of the freedom movement, after the experience of black searches for identity, after young white people had been brought into a new life of working for change, America could never go back to the days

By revealing the contradictions that had been part of America from the beginning—that is, the unfair treatment of African Americans in a country founded on the principles of equality and justice—civil rights activists transformed the nation. In 1960, these protesters boycotted stores with segreagated lunch counters in Tallahassee, Florida.

before Montgomery, to the times before the *Brown* decision.

But the change was greater than anyone could have imagined in the most powerful dreams of the 1950s and 1960s. Eventually, Americans witnessed on television the rising of new liberation and pro-democracy movements that seemed to sweep over the globe from Beijing to Berlin in the 1970s and 1980s. We saw how the participants in these movements often marched into their struggles to the music of "We Shall Overcome," sometimes facing batallions of armed troops with their songs and their courage. The message and the power of the black freedom movement could not be contained in America.

So Unita Blackwell, one of the most committed freedom workers in Mississippi in the 1960s, was not exaggerating when she looked back from the 1980s and took stock: "We didn't have anything and we changed the world." Blackwell knew that although most of the South's freedom workers had very little of what is usually considered necessary eqiupment for change—money, political power, and social status—the army of hope did have something. These people had dreams of new possibilities. And they had a determination to work for those dreams. They had courage, a courage that grew as they moved forward on a mission that sometimes seemed impossible.

Blackwell knew that they had each other and they found ways to hold on to their sisters and brothers, through the most dangerous times. And at the base of it all, they had a deep faith in God. They believed that their work for freedom, justice, and democracy was in harmony with the intentions of God, and they refused to be moved, refused to be turned around, refused to lose hope.

By the time Blackwell made her statement, she knew what freedom and democracy workers all over the world had learned. And that was the truth of an old African-American song: "Freedom is a constant struggle."

CHRONOLOGY

AUGUST 14, 1945
World War II ends.

JUNE 3, 1946
U.S. Supreme Court bans segregation in interstate bus travel in *Morgan* v. *Virginia.*

APRIL 9, 1947
Civil rights groups organize the first Freedom Rides to test compliance with bus integration law.

APRIL 10, 1947
Jackie Robinson of the Brooklyn Dodgers becomes the first African American to play major league baseball.

JULY 26, 1948
President Harry S. Truman signs an executive order ending segregation of the armed forces.

MAY 17, 1954
U.S. Supreme Court rules in *Brown* v. *Board of Education* that school segregation is illegal.

DECEMBER 1, 1955
In Montgomery, Alabama, a bus boycott begins after Rosa Parks is arrested for refusing to give up her seat on a bus to a white man.

NOVEMBER 13, 1956
U.S. Supreme Court rules in *Gayle* v. *Browder* that segregation in Montgomery's buses is illegal.

SEPTEMBER 1957
President Dwight D. Eisenhower orders federal troops to enforce school desegregation in Little Rock, Arkansas.

FEBRUARY 1960
Students stage a sit-in to protest segregated lunch counters in Greensboro, North Carolina.

MAY 14, 1961
Freedom Riders are attacked in Alabama.

SEPTEMBER 30, 1962
Riots erupt after James Meredith becomes the first black student to enroll at the University of Mississippi.

MAY 3, 1963
Police in Birmingham, Alabama, use dogs and fire hoses to attack civil rights marchers.

JUNE 11, 1963
Governor George Wallace stands in the door of the University of Alabama to prevent a black student from enrolling.

JUNE 12, 1963
Civil rights leader Medgar Evers is slain in Jackson, Mississippi.

AUGUST 28, 1963
Martin Luther King, Jr., leads 250,000 Americans in the March on Washington, D.C.

SPETEMBER 15, 1963

Four schoolgirls are killed when bomb explodes at the Sixteenth Street Baptist Church in Birmingham.

NOVEMBER 22, 1963

President John F. Kennedy is assassinated in Dallas, Texas.

JUNE 20, 1964

During Freedom Summer, 1,000 civil rights volunteers go to Mississippi.

AUGUST 20, 1964

President Lyndon Johnson signs the Economic Opportunity Act.

JULY 2, 1964

President Lyndon Johnson signs Civil Rights Act.

DECEMBER 10, 1964

Martin Luther King, Jr., receives the Nobel Peace Prize.

FEBRUARY 1965

Malcolm X is shot and killed in New York City.

MARCH 7, 1965

Civil rights marchers in Selma, Alabama, are clubbed and gassed by police.

MARCH 9, 1965

Under the protection of federal troops, civil rights marchers complete the trek from Selma to Montgomery.

AUGUST 11, 1965

Rebellion in the Watts section of Los Angeles results in 34 people dead and $35 million in property damage.

JUNE 26, 1966

At a civil rights rally in Mississippi, Stokely Carmichael launches the Black Power movement.

JULY 1967

Riots in urban areas leave scores dead and many neighborhoods in ruins.

OCTOBER 2, 1967

Thurgood Marshall is sworn in as the first African-American justice of the U.S. Supreme Court.

FEBRUARY 29, 1968

The Kerner Commission warns that America is becoming "two societies—one black, one white—separate and unequal."

APRIL 4, 1968

Martin Luther King, Jr., is assassinated in Memphis, Tennessee.

JUNE 19, 1968

The Poor People's Campaign brings 50,000 demonstrators to Washington.

FURTHER READING

GENERAL AFRICAN-AMERICAN HISTORY

Bennett, Lerone, Jr. *Before the Mayflower: A History of Black America.* 6th rev. ed. New York: Viking Penguin, 1988.

———. *The Shaping of Black America.* New York: Viking Penguin, 1993.

Cone, James. *Martin and Malcolm and America.* Maryknoll, N.Y.: Orbis, 1991.

Franklin, John H., and Alfred A. Moss, Jr. *From Slavery to Freedom: A History of Negro Americans.* 6th ed. New York: Knopf, 1987.

Gates, Henry L., Jr. *A Chronology of African-American History from 1445–1980.* New York: Amistad, 1980.

Giddings, Paula. *When and Where I Enter: The Impact of Black Women on Race and Sex in America.* New York: Bantam, 1985.

Harding, Vincent. *There is a River: The Black Struggle for Freedom in America.* San Diego: Harcourt Brace, 1981.

Hine, Darlene C., et al., eds. *Black Women in America.* Brooklyn, N.Y.: Carlson, 1993.

Meltzer, Milton. *The Black Americans: A History in Their Own Words.* Rev. ed. New York: HarperCollins, 1984.

Quarles, Benjamin. *The Negro in the Making of America.* 3rd ed. New York: Macmillan, 1987.

CIVIL RIGHTS ERA

Lincoln, C. Eric. *The Black Muslims in America.* Grand Rapids, Mich.: Eerdmans, 1994.

Patterson, James T. *Grand Expectations: The United States, 1945–1974.* New York: Oxford University Press, 1996.

Wofford, Harris. *Of Kennedys and Kings: Making Sense of the Sixties.* New York: Farrar Straus Giroux, 1980.

CIVIL RIGHTS MOVEMENT

Archer, Jules. *They Had a Dream: The Civil Rights Struggle, from Frederick Douglass to Marcus Garvey to Martin Luther King, Jr. and Malcolm X.* New York: Viking, 1993.

Branch, Taylor. *Parting the Waters: America in the King Years, 1954–1963.* New York: Simon & Schuster, 1988.

Bullard, Sara. *Free at Last: A History of the Civil Rights Movement and Those Who Died in the Struggle.* New York: Oxford University Press, 1993.

Carawan, Guy, and Candie Carawan. *Freedom Is a Constant Struggle: Songs of the Freedom Movement.* New York: Oak Publications, 1968.

Carson, Claybourne. *In Struggle: SNCC and the Black Awakening of the 1960s.* Cambridge: Harvard University Press, 1981.

Carson, Claybourne, et al. *The Eyes on the Prize Civil Rights Reader.* New York: Penguin, 1991.

Chafe, William H. *Civilities and Civil Rights: Greensboro, North Carolina, and the Black Struggle for Freedom.* New York: Oxford University Press, 1980.

Cleghorn, Reese, and Pat Watters. *Climbing Jacob's Ladder: The Arrival of Negroes in Southern Politics.* New York: Harcourt, Brace & World, 1967.

Couto, Richard A. *Ain't Gonna Let Nobody Turn Me Round: The Pursuit of Racial Justice in the Rural South.* Philadelphia: Temple University Press, 1991.

Crawford, Vicki, Jacqueline Anne Rouse, and Barbara Woods, eds. *Women in the Civil Rights Movement: Trailblazers and Torchbearers, 1941–1965.* Bloomington: Indiana University Press, 1993.

Egerton, John. *Speak Now Against the Day: The Generation Before the Civil Rights Movement in the South.* New York: Knopf, 1994.

Fairclough, Adam. *To Redeem the Soul of America: The Southern Christian Leadership Conference and Martin Luther King, Jr.* Athens: University of Georgia Press, 1987.

Forman, James. *The Making of Black Revolutionaries.* New York: Macmillan, 1972.

Grant, Joanne, ed. *Black Protest: History, Documents, and Analyses, 1619 to the Present.* New York: St. Martin's, 1970.

Hampton, Henry, and Steve Fayer, with Sarah Flynn. *Voices of Freedom: An Oral History of the Civil Rights Movement from the 1950s through the 1980s.* New York: Bantam, 1990.

Harding, Vincent. *Hope and History: Why We Must Share the Story of the Movement.* Maryknoll, N.Y.: Orbis, 1990. Haskins, James. *The Freedom Rides: Journey for Justice.* New York: Hyperion, 1995.

Hughes, Langston. *Fight for Freedom: The Story of the NAACP.* New York: Berkley, 1962.

Kapur, Sudarshan. *Raising Up a Prophet: The African-American Encounter With Gandhi.* Boston: Beacon Press, 1992.

King, Martin Luther, Jr. *Stride Toward Freedom.* New York: Harper & Row, 1958.

———. *Trumpet of Conscience.* New York: Harper & Row, 1968.

———. *Where Do We Go from Here: Chaos or Community?* New York: Harper & Row, 1967.

———. *Why We Can't Wait.* New York: Harper & Row, 1964.

Kluger, Richard. *Simple Justice: The History of Brown v. Board of Education and Black America's Struggle for Equality.* New York: Knopf, 1975.

Lawson, Stephen. *Running for Freedom: Civil Rights and Black Politics in America Since 1941.* New York: McGraw-Hill, 1991.

Lewis, Anthony. *Portrait of a Decade: The Second American Revolution.* New York: Random House, 1964.

Lomax, Louis E. *The Negro Revolt.* New York: Harper & Row, 1962.

Lowery, Charles D., and John F. Marszalek, eds. *Encyclopedia of African-American Civil Rights.* New York: Greenwood, 1992.

Lyon, Danny. *Memories of the Southern Civil Rights Movement.* Chapel Hill: University of North Carolina Press, 1992.

Meier, August, and Elliot Rudwick. *CORE: A Study in the Civil Rights Movement, 1942–1968.* New York: Oxford University Press, 1973.

Morris, Aldon D. *The Origins of the Civil Rights Movement.* New York: Free Press, 1984.

O'Reilly, Kenneth. *"Racial Matters": The FBI's Secret File on Black America, 1960–1972.* New York: Free Press, 1989.

Payne, Charles M. *I've Got the Light of Freedom.* Berkeley: University of California Press, 1995.

Peck, James. *Freedom Ride.* New York: Simon & Schuster, 1962.

President's Committee on Civil Rights. *To Secure These Rights.* Washington: U.S. Government Printing Office, 1947.

Raines, Howell. *My Soul is Rested: The Story of the Civil Rights Movement in the Deep South.* New York: Viking Penguin, 1977.

Reiser, Bob, and Pete Seeger. *Everybody Says Freedom: A History of the Civil Rights Movement in Songs and Pictures.* New York: Norton, 1989.

Sitkoff, Harvard. *The Struggle for Black Equality.* New York: Hill & Wang, 1993.

Skolnick, Jerome. *The Politics of Protest.* New York: Ballantine, 1969.

Sugarman, Tracy. *Stranger at the Gates: A Summer in Mississippi.* New York: Hill & Wang, 1966.

Weisbrot, Robert. *Freedom Bound: A History of America's Civil Rights Movement.* New York: Norton, 1990.

Williams, Juan. *Eyes on the Prize: America's Civil Rights Years, 1954–1965.* New York: Penguin, 1988.

Young, Andrew. *An Easy Burden: The Civil Rights Movement and the Transformation of America.* New York: HarperCollins, 1996.

Zinn, Howard. *SNCC: The New Abolitionists.* Boston: Beacon Press, 1964.

AUTOBIOGRAPHIES AND BIOGRAPHIES

Anderson, Jervis. *Bayard Rustin: Troubles I've Seen, a Biography.* New York: HarperCollins, 1997.

Baraka, Amiri. *The Autobiography of LeRoi Jones/Amiri Baraka.* New York: Freundlich Books, 1984.

Bennett, Lerone, Jr. *What Manner of Man: A Biography of Martin Luther King, Jr.* Chicago: Johnson, 1964.

Burner, Eric. *And Gently He Shall Lead Them: Robert Parris Moses and Civil Rights In Mississippi.* New York: New York University Press, 1994.

Carmichael, Stokely. *Black Power: The Politics of Liberation in America.* New York: Vintage, 1992.

Carson, Claybourne. *Malcolm X, The FBI File.* New York: Carroll & Graf, 1991.

Carson, Claybourne, ed. *The Papers of Martin Luther King, Jr.* Berkeley: University of California Press, 1992.

Clark, Septima P. *Echo In My Soul.* New York: Dutton, 1962.

———. *Ready From Within.* Navarro, Calif.: Wild Trees Press, 1986.

Dallard, Shyrlee. *Ella Baker: A Leader behind the Scenes.* Englewood Cliffs, N.J.: Silver Burdett, 1990.

Garrow, David. *Bearing the Cross: Martin Luther King, Jr., and the Southern Christian Leadership Conference.* New York: Morrow, 1986.

Goldman, Peter. *The Death and Life of Malcolm X.* New York: Harper & Row, 1973.

Hamilton, Charles V. *Adam Clayton Powell, Jr.* New York: Atheneum, 1991.

Harding, Vincent. *Martin Luther King: The Inconvenient Hero.* Maryknoll, N.Y.: Orbis, 1996.

Jakoubek, Robert. *Martin Luther King, Jr.* New York: Chelsea House, 1989.

Johnson, Jacqueline. *Stokely Carmichael: The Story of Black Power.* Englewood Cliffs, N.J.: Silver Burdett, 1990.

King, Coretta Scott. *My Life With Martin Luther King, Jr.* New York: Holt, Rinehart & Winston, 1969.

King, Martin Luther, Sr., with Clayton Riley. *Daddy King.* New York: Morrow, 1980.

Lewis, David L. *King: A Critical Biography.* New York: Praeger, 1970.

Malcolm X, with the assistance of Alex Haley. *The Autobiography of Malcolm X.* New York: Grove Press, 1965.

Mills, Kay. *This Little Light of Mine: The Life of Fannie Lou Hamer.* New York: Dutton, 1993.

Oates, Stephen B. *Let the Trumpet Sound: The Life of Martin Luther King, Jr.* New York: Harper & Row, 1982.

Rummel, Jack. *Malcolm X.* New York: Chelsea House, 1989.

Washington, James M. *A Testament of Hope: The Essential Writings of Martin Luther King, Jr.* New York: Harper & Row, 1986.

Wilkins, Roy, with Tom Mathews. *Standing Fast: The Autobiography of Roy Wilkins.* New York: Viking, 1982.

INDEX

ACKNOWLEDGMENTS

I am very grateful for the support I received from the Oxford team that helped to make this book possible, even when they had to contend with my procrastination and constant failures to meet deadlines and to stay within word limits: Nancy Toff of Oxford balanced patience and a sense of urgency at the right times. In addition to their work as series editors, Robin Kelley and Earl Lewis graciously took on major responsibility for developing chapters 7 and 8. In Denver, my brother, friend, and comrade, Sudarshan Kapur, was also of great assistance. Shirley Kaaz, my secretary, responded with skill, kindness, and dependability to many urgent calls for help. And in their own special ways, Rosemarie Freeney Harding and Rachel Harding, my wife and daughter, my co-workers and teachers, stood with me and strengthened me. I am grateful.

PICTURE CREDITS

AP/Wide World Photos: 49, 84; Currie Ballard, historian, Langston University: 91; Corbis-Bettmann: 130; Frank Driggs/Corbis-Bettmann: 22; Florida State Archives: 62, 65, 67, 76, 83, 87, 111, 183; Hampton University Museum, Hampton, Virginia. Charles White, detail from *The Contribution of the Negro to Democracy in America*, 1943: 9; Hirshorn Museum and Sculpture Garden, Smithsonian Institution, Museum Purchase, 1977, Lee Stalsworth, photographer: cover; LBJ Library Collection: 134, 152; Library of Congress: 20, 21, 24, 35, 42, 55, 70, 73, 74, 75, 79, 101, 115, 143, 144, 146, 160, 162, 164, 173, 180; © Danny Lyon/Magnum Photos, Inc.: 95; courtesy Morehouse College: 37, 38; National Archives: 2, 12, 13, 15, 131, 175; courtesy NAACP Department of Public Relations: 34; New York Public Library Picture Collection: 166; Schomburg Center for Research in Black Culture, New York Public Library, Astor, Lenox and Tilden Foundations: 8, 19, 32, 82, 126; Steve Schapiro/Black Star: 118; Temple University Libraries, Urban Archives: 16, 149; Tuskegee University Archives: 28; UPI/Corbis-Bettmann: 18, 25, 27, 29, 31, 40, 45, 48, 53, 57, 59, 69, 93, 98, 105, 120, 122, 124, 125, 133, 136, 137, 138, 139, 140, 142, 155, 157, 168, 169, 170, 177, 178; photography by Ernest Withers, courtesy Panopticon Gallery, Boston: 60 (negative number 17), 89 (negative number 20), 108 (negative number 31).

VINCENT HARDING
◇ ◇ ◇

Vincent Harding is professor of religion and social transformation at the Iliff School of Theology at the University of Denver. He is the author of, among many other publications, *There Is a River,* a history of the pre–Civil War African-American struggle for freedom, and *Hope and History,* which addresses the lessons to be learned from teaching the story of the modern African-American freedom movement. From 1961 to 1964, Harding worked as an activist, teacher, and negotiator for the Southern freedom movement. From 1968 to 1970, he was director of the Martin Luther King, Jr., Library Documentation Project and the Martin Luther King, Jr., Memorial Center in Atlanta, and from 1969 to 1974, he served as director of the Atlanta-based Institute of the Black World, an organization that he helped to found. Harding was senior academic adviser to the PBS television series "Eyes on the Prize," about the civil rights movement. He and his family have been actively engaged in justice and peace movements in this country and overseas.

ROBIN D. G. KELLEY
◇ ◇ ◇

Robin D. G. Kelley is professor of history and Africana studies at New York University. He previously taught history and African-American studies at the University of Michigan. He is the author of *Hammer and Hoe: Alabama Communists during the Great Depression,* which received the Eliot Rudwick Prize of the Organization of American Historians and was named Outstanding Book on Human Rights by the Gustavus Myers Center for the Study of Human Rights in the United States. Professor Kelley is also the author of *Race Rebels: Culture, Politics, and the Black Working Class* and co-editor of *Imagining Home: Class, Culture, and Nationalism in the African Diaspora.*

EARL LEWIS
◇ ◇ ◇

Earl Lewis is professor of history and Afroamerican studies at the University of Michigan. He served as director of the university's Center for Afroamerican and African Studies from 1990 to 1993. Professor Lewis is the author of *In Their Own Interests: Race, Class and Power in Twentieth Century Norfolk* and co-author of *Blacks in the Industrial Age: A Documentary History.*